THE ELEMENT OF IRONY
IN ENGLISH LITERATURE

THE
ELEMENT OF IRONY
IN
ENGLISH LITERATURE

AN ESSAY
BY
F. MᶜD. C. TURNER

Donaldson Bye-Fellow of Magdalene College
Cambridge

CAMBRIDGE
at the University Press
MCMXXVI

CAMBRIDGE
UNIVERSITY PRESS

University Printing House, Cambridge CB2 8BS, United Kingdom

Published in the United States of America by Cambridge University Press, New York

Cambridge University Press is part of the University of Cambridge.

It furthers the University's mission by disseminating knowledge in the pursuit of
education, learning and research at the highest international levels of excellence.

www.cambridge.org
Information on this title: www.cambridge.org/9781107426597

First published 1926
First paperback edition 2014

A catalogue record for this publication is available from the British Library

ISBN 978-1-107-42659-7 Paperback

PREFACE

This essay was awarded the Le Bas prize in 1924 and is now, rather behind time, I fear, published in accordance with the regulations of that prize. With the permission, and in some cases on the advice, of the Adjudicators, certain alterations and additions have been made. In particular, much of the last chapter and some of chapter IV is new.

But I feel that little improvement has been made; the essay remains, as it was in its original form, quite inadequate, if anything approaching a comprehensive review of English irony is expected. Many authors, famous in our literature, and admirable in their use of irony, are unmentioned here, and even Gibbon, the very name that must spring first to the mind of an Englishman when irony is discussed, receives but scant attention. But I must let the essay explain itself: the only irony which seems to me to have been at any time so characteristic as to deserve to be considered an element in our literature is the kind that in this essay I have called prophetic; and Gibbon's irony is not of this kind. Of many English poets, indeed, the same cannot be said; but in so short a book it seemed impossible to attempt an exhaustive survey even of prophetic irony, and I thought it best to confine myself to works of prose.

F. M^cD. C. T.

December 1925

CONTENTS

CHAPTER I

THE MEANING OF IRONY

Scientific methods are at once the friend and the tormentor of the essay-writer; they allow him too little and too much. They will, for instance, forbid him to enlarge himself upon the subject of Romance, until he has defined the meaning of that elusive word; but, so soon as he bows to their will, their relentlessness is vanished away; they permit him a complete liberty of definition, for they are concerned with consistency rather than with the truth in words. Indeed, to the scientific mind such an expression as 'the truth in words' may well seem a manifest symptom of disordered thought, for words are no more knowledge than a milestone is distance. And yet the man of letters, the artist in words, will continue to wonder whether the matter is so easily resolved. He is for many reasons provoked by the scientist; in the first place, the methods of the latter remind him too much of Humpty-Dumpty. But whereas Humpty-Dumpty tells us 'when I make a word do a lot of work like that, I always pay it extra,' the scientist says nothing of the sort; indeed, he would laugh at the idea, and his style shows no sign of any such reasonable generosity; his poor words are tired and overwrought. The irritation which the scientist causes is a very just one, for he is condemned not for his science, but for his lack of science. When in the past he cried in alarm that thought was becoming enslaved by speech and that man must show his independence by making words his servants and assigning to each a strict meaning, he was giving voice to a fear and to a sentiment that the literary artist is ever ready to proclaim. But at this point the scientist forgot himself: he omitted to add, and in practice ignored the fact, that this cry of independence was a call for concerted action, and not a declaration of individual licence. He forgot, too, that words have emerged chastened and clarified by the mental strife and unerring taste of great men, that to a single word, thus purified, can become attached something of the illumination with which genius has converted adventurous intuition into demonstrable conviction, and that the elect amongst words cannot be deprived of the meaning they held in the day of victory, without grievous loss to the language to which they belong.

These things escaped the scientist when, in the swiftness of his progress, it seemed a convenience to be an individualist in language; but confusion descended upon his heedlessness and he long since resolved to set his house in order and to clear the ways of knowledge by the redemption of violated words. Our business is not to examine the effects of this laudable conversion, but to turn from these speculations to matters more closely connected with our subject. The connection is not obscure; for if ever a word has suffered, and suffers, abuse in common speech, it is 'irony.' It is a word which has never had the good fortune to become one of the elect in spite of the fact that it is indispensable. And this ill luck it owes to its meaning, which, although exact in essence, is in practice composite, belonging to several phenomena, united only by a single common tie. The

2

essential nature of irony is to be found in this common factor, but here again circumstances are adverse to exact definitions. For irony has an emotional element which it is so hard to mistake, that attention is diverted to the dramatic setting wherein the ironic spirit seems most at home, and it escapes notice that a thing emotionally clear is often intellectually abstruse. Thus for lack of analysis the word suffers abuse, and even where it is saved this degradation, it has no option but to be escorted by a variety of qualifying adjectives to denote the different phenomena wherein it resides, and so we hear of 'dramatic irony,' 'the irony of Fate,' 'Socratic irony,' quite apart from the simple but elusive thing that we denote when we use the word without qualification.

Irony in human experience is roughly of three kinds: there is, in the first place, 'the irony of Fate,' so called because the perceiver of the irony possesses powers of correlating human affairs and of knowing the future beyond the capabilities of man, except when he is assisted by particular circumstances; there is 'simple irony,' wherein one man speaks ironically to another, and he, the victim, even if he does not perceive an exact double meaning, is conscious of a sly assault upon him; finally, there is 'dramatic irony,' which must be subdivided. In its simplest form, dramatic irony is a matter for two people who have no connection with each other: one person, the onlooker, perceives another acting in a manner which is the result of ignorance, on the part of the actor, of certain facts known to the onlooker. But

3

more often dramatic irony assumes a more complex form: *A* speaks to, or acts towards, *B* in such fashion as to convey an outer and superficial meaning to *B*, but an inner and more fundamental meaning to *C*, an onlooker; and this, again, assumes a different nature, according to whether *A* is the conscious perpetrator of the irony, or the tool of circumstances, or of some fourth person, *D*: the one essential which unites these various kinds of dramatic irony, is the presence of a disinterested spectator, whose knowledge of the affair embraces that of all the actors. But when this spectator, the perceiver of the irony, is in no way responsible for the ironic forces at work, he bears witness to that irony of Fate which human agencies have encouraged.

The fact remains that in all these situations there seems to be a spirit at work which we agree in calling ironical; the only difference between the irony of Fate and any other irony being that in the irony of Fate we are attributing events, the correlation of which seems to betray an ironical spirit outside and controlling human and natural behaviour, to the agency of that mysterious being. The irony that is the conscious product of the human mind has been called 'simple' irony where one man 'ironises' another through the direct medium of speech, and 'dramatic' where one man makes use of circumstances to entertain or represent ironical notions of the behaviour of another, either by speech or action, or the conscious or unconscious agency of a third person. It will be clear that of these types 'simple' irony can alone be considered an element in literature, for it alone of them is exclusively concerned with the conveyance of thought in speech. Both dramatic irony and the irony of Fate are elemental in drama, but in literature they are only topics, for literature is not *per se* related to the idea of drama, but only to the expression of this idea, as of all other ideas, in speech.

The scope of this essay, then, will not extend beyond the consideration of those utterances which contain in themselves the full extent of the ironic idea they convey: for, given suitable circumstances, almost any remark could be made the agent of irony. There are cases where such circumstances are entirely literary, and from which would arise such ironies as may be contained in parody for instance. But for the sake of simplicity, and also because the subject is a large one, we shall confine ourselves here to direct and simple irony. In fiction and history the situation is slightly more complex, because the author sometimes uses his *dramatis personae* to give voice to his own irony; but this should not prove a very dangerous stumbling block, for to confuse this with dramatic irony would be to assume the relations between an author and the characters of his pen to be the same as those existing between one living person and another.

It must now become our task to examine the mental attitude of the ironist, to discover what is the outlook, what are the purposes, and what the emotions, that result in ironical utterance. What the ironist in fact achieves is the sudden projection of something vividly before us, and we are precipitated into passing judgment

5

upon it not so much intellectually as immediately by the value-sense that is within us. And when the thing so projected is a thought or an argument, what we are called upon to examine is the inherent *worthiness* of that thought. We must satisfy ourselves, for instance, that it does not disclose a mind restricted by prejudice or agitated by pride, but one that moves, for the most part, freely, and is sustained by the saving grace of a sense of proportion, which is, perhaps, none other than this same value-sense that irony prompts us to exercise. Thus Plato, in the beginning of the *Republic*, does not seek directly to ironise the idea that justice is the right of the stronger over the weaker, for strength can mean many things, and the idea is not unworthy of our consideration; what he is very ready to ironise is the mental attitude of a man like Thrasymachus.

Such considerations raise the vexed question of the relation of irony with that 'enmity complex' which in literature at any rate appears so frequently and so openly to accompany it. The appeal that the ironist makes to our judgment owes its efficacy to its suddenness; we are surprised into it and cannot escape to take thought. Now a sudden assessment of thought or behaviour will be primarily moral; intuitive evaluation is concerned with fundamentals, with beauty, with goodness, and with truth. Of course the immediateness of this appeal varies greatly with the irony employed; but even in his most playful mood the ironist is, whether consciously or not, making such an appeal. When we say that a thing is absurd, that stricture is seldom a

6

purely rational one; but it need not be the less true for that reason. The ironist is always asking us to observe the absurdity of things; his methods are not suitable for the revelation of what is admirable. The process of ironic exposure is an unpleasant one, and fortunately admirable qualities do not require it. Hence it follows that irony is employed as an engine of destructive criticism, and as such has been dragged into the worst regions of personal strife in literature, and has become connected with too much that is spiteful and vindictive. Yet it should be remembered, in the first place, that irony should be employed against thoughts and actions rather than against particular individuals who indulge in such thoughts and actions; and, secondly, that direct irony is a means and not an end; it is a method of criticism, and not an experience of critical thought.

Moreover, if enmity, or at any rate a disapproval that has amounted to irritation, be too often an incentive to ironical utterance, this disapproval, however hostile, must be mixed with a more admirable desire to expose the truth, to ridicule the ridiculous, and, if necessary, abominate the abominable. Irony may spring from a lust of conquest, but the enemy is to be convicted by Truth. She declares judgment and is the real conqueror; the achievement and delight of the human combatant is to force the enemy before that solemn arbiter, to expose him there suddenly, unready and unexpectant. To ignore this fact and to define irony as malicious ambiguity of speech is entirely misleading. For irony is an engine of destructive criticism in only a very

7

limited sense; the ironist himself does not pass judgment but appeals to our sense of truth and justice to do so. If truth be judge when irony prosecutes, it follows that nothing that is excellent can in this way be hurt; on the contrary, just because the method is a harsh one, our indignation will go forth against the ironist himself, if it shall appear that his victim is unjustly arraigned and undeserving of our summary jurisdiction.

The ambiguity of ironical speech is a topic which demands a little consideration. Many people have been misled into a belief that this ambiguity is a vehicle of bitterness and nothing more. Thus, in his essay on comedy, Meredith writes: 'If instead of falling foul of the ridiculous person with a satiric rod to make him writhe and shriek aloud, you prefer to sting him under a semi-caress, by which he shall in his anguish be rendered dubious whether indeed anything has hurt him, you are an engine of irony.' But the bitterness of this ambiguity is purely incidental; the ambiguity itself is a method of criticism. Indeed, the word 'ambiguity' is highly misleading, since it adopts the point of view of the victim only. The ironist is concerned far more with incongruity than with ambiguity. He places ridiculous things amongst the dignified, bad amongst good, and false amongst true, so that their ridiculousness, badness and falseness may become obvious to all sensible people. But he does not explain that this is what he is doing; it is not necessary, and it might spoil the sudden clarity that he hopes to awaken in our minds by means of these juxtapositions. And if it happens that certain people who had believed the ridiculous to be dignified or the bad to be good begin to have misgivings and find his language bitterly ambiguous, that is their fault. Yet the ironist should deal with them as gently as he can, for without them there would be no need for irony. It is a poor achievement to expose what everyone despises. These things the ironist not infrequently forgets.

Thus, while a hasty appeal to experience might tempt one to define an ironical utterance as a veiled attack wherein the sting dependent on truth for its efficacy is enwrapped in a superficial and insincere sympathy, a more detached observer might be content to declare that *irony in speech is a form of destructive criticism that enforces an immediate judgment upon something by placing it without comment in a position to which it should not aspire*, but to which we may add, it probably has been aspiring. In other words, the ironist attempts to convict the foolish of their folly by appearing to accept the logical deductions arising from it, and by solemnly parading absurdities before our eyes.

Perhaps we have been considering irony too exclusively in its most primitive form; we have thought of it as a weapon confined to the execution of relentless hostilities. Although in actual life, as in the history of literature, irony not infrequently experiences some difficulty in entirely freeing itself from the gloomy atmosphere of war, like most other forms of criticism, while unpleasant in its most personal aspect, it becomes less offensive and far more versatile when it is used with detachment and its personal venom is reduced to a minimum. Nor need it only be exercised against such follies as are contemptible and spring from disagreeable people; there are many amiable weaknesses and laughable errors in human life that invite the mockery of a gentle and a playful irony. Thus irony can grow almost benign, becoming, as Meredith said, the humour of satire. Yet its laughter is never the laughter of true humour; it can cast off fierce ill-will, but it can never assume the positive charity that humour demands. It remains like a soldier playing at war with a child, allowing no quarter even in the game of pretence, and in these homely regions irony is apt to move with a tread that is somewhat stiff and heavy. But soldiers not infrequently learn docility, and so, let us hope, may irony. We walk, however, on a smooth and polished floor supported by the goodwill which is the first necessity of civilised life: through this, irony may at any time break, slipping clumsily, and drag us with it on a compulsory visit to the dingy caverns of 'the state of Nature.'

Thus it will appear that the history of irony in polite literature is a hazardous one and the perils that beset an intruder attend upon it. The god of irony, as might be expected, is a jealous god: he causes his votaries, be they ever so little imprudent, to appear odious in the sight of man. The ironist has no alternative between success and such failure as will invest him before the public eye with the insignificance of meanness. It is this fact which gives our subject its especial interest, for the successful use of irony is always an artistic victory: triumphant intrusion is a very great achievement. So far as literature is concerned, the history of irony is the history of good manners.

The uses of irony in literature fall roughly into two categories, but there is no fixed boundary between them. It can be used as Swift, Milton and Defoe have used it, and be made the instrument of prophetic utterance and the major criticisms of man by man. Such irony will be called 'prophetic irony' throughout this essay. Irony has also its smaller and milder uses; Gibbon and Jane Austen are more concerned with the details of human folly as found in individual action than with public error or general depravity, and their irony is more concerned with laughter than with preaching. They do not plunge into irony, but use the occasion when it arises. Such irony is a commentary rather than a critical structure, and we shall speak of it as 'little irony.' It can be used in most forms of literature, but it arises most naturally in works which are mainly of a narrative sort, in fiction and history and biography.

In this essay we shall be chiefly concerned with the more formal irony of the public moralist, for it is prophetic irony which, as it seems to us, has had a particular vogue in this country, and might with some justice be called an element in English literature. We shall endeavour to trace the progress of this irony both in respect to those who are most conspicuous as producers of it, and to the general spirit of the age that seemed to welcome and demand it. In dealing with these great ironists we shall try to produce examples that will be illustrative of their work, but if quotations seem to be given rather sparingly, it will perhaps be allowed that irony, as much as anything, suffers from being dragged out of its context. Especially is this the case with slighter, and, in a sense, finer pieces of irony, and in the concluding chapter, in which, under the title of 'Irony in Narrative,' we shall deal with 'little irony,' and such irony as cannot deserve the name 'prophetic irony,' it has been thought best to abandon all attempt at quotation, and to treat the subject in a more general way.

The general scheme of this essay and the reason for the divisions that will be made will, it is hoped, become clear in the course of reading. It should perhaps be emphasized that no attempt can here be made to trace the whole course of irony in English literature; such a subject would demand a treatment far beyond the scope of this essay. For the same reason it will be found that, even in the period with which we shall deal in particular, we shall confine ourselves to those ironists whose works seem to be significant and influential in the progress of irony in this country.

A start which is not at the beginning involves an exercise of choice which must, in the nature of things, be somewhat arbitrary; and our decision to take the era of civil strife, the Miltonic age in literature, as the earliest period for consideration in this essay cannot escape the charge. But the reasons for this decision may best be left to the next chapter.

CHAPTER II

MILTON AND THE DAWN OF THE AGE OF IRONY

In discussing a general topic in English literature one cannot ignore the Elizabethan age without regret, nor yet without seriously imperilling, not only the completeness, but the very structure of his achievement. Nor in the present case is it possible to maintain that irony did not exist in our literature until the Rebellion, although it was but faintly apparent; and the omission of so fertile an age as the Elizabethan cannot be passed over without some explanation. Fortunately, it will not be necessary to make a digression in self-defence; the point in question is too germane to our subject.

The Elizabethan age was the consummation of a civilisation which had been growing up in this country since 1485 when the Tudor accession put an end to internal dissension. This culture did not show signs of decadence in the reigns of the first two Stuarts; what happened was simply that the initial period of intense creative activity had given place to a quieter time, when imagination did not wither, but creation to a certain extent gave way to criticism and a wider diffusion of literary appreciation took the place of the pre-eminent genius of a few. In those generous days, expression attained to a directness and a dignity such as are seldom to be found; moreover, criticism assumed that impersonal aspect which is always the sign of serenity. Hence it is not surprising that irony is more in evidence at that earlier period of lively social movement and individual prowess, which we associate with such men as Sir Thomas More and Dean Colet, and far less active when the individualism of the Renaissance gave way to the national enthusiasm that characterises the reign of Queen Elizabeth. But with the dawn of the seventeenth century a new factor arose; it became apparent that the unnatural severity of the Puritan spirit would prove a deadly enemy to much that was best in literature, while as yet the artistic vision of Englishmen had not begun to fail them; and when to this sombre outlook was added the dreadful bitterness and the intellectual confusion of the Civil War, we have the dismal spectacle of a nation's art succumbing not to its own weariness and exhaustion, but destroyed in midsummer by the storms and blizzards of external circumstances.

No age, as we think, has been more misjudged than the Restoration period; we think of the people of those times as decadent and persecuting, immoral and intolerant. Many were none of those things, and as for the many who were, we forget the cause. The Englishman born in the reign of James I was born at a time when it might seem that a golden age was at hand for art and literature, and the cultivated circles who cared for these things; a time had come, not, perhaps, of heroic creation, but of secure and joyful appreciation, a time when thought was lyrical; and throughout the country, masks, self-conscious and stiffly pastoral on the surface, expressed, nevertheless, the gratification of hearts not doubting that summer had come to stay. Then, suddenly, the cloud discernible at Hampton Court assumed gigantic proportions; innumerable potentialities vanished in the storm, and there settled upon people that peculiar sense of bitterness that belongs to the destruction of artistic freedom and the interruption of spontaneous acknowledgment of beauty. They were, indeed, the victims of the bitterest stroke of life's irony, when art and religious enthusiasm became embroiled through the intolerance of both; and, as if in admission of their own shortcomings and the unbending harshness of their fate, there entered the hearts of these unhappy people such a bitterness that for a long time the most common form of criticism was with them the fiercest and most vindictive type of ironical utterance; for the outward prosperity of the Restoration mocked their knowledge of the unrecoverable. Thus it is that the period from the Civil Wars to the time when the mild Addison brought again a more kindly element into our literature might almost be called the Age of Irony, although, with the notable exception of Swift, it is not at this time that the best examples of English irony are to be found. For irony should be an emergency weapon; it is most successful when it is used most sparingly; where it is most common, it will also be most debased.

The bewildering days of Charles II and his portentous successor were neither natural nor healthy; no Age of Irony could be. The actors on that delirious stage were moving 'in a world not realised'; their mock hilarity served only to conceal the wounds that hampered them within. The nation had received a shock that left it stunned and lifeless for a generation; imagination was rendered senseless and spontaneity vanished; people went through life mechanically and their mirth was laboured; their wild extravagances sprang from the hysteria that alternates with lethargy in neurotic conditions. The result of this depressing state of affairs is that the literature of that age seems strangely remote from us to-day; the men who produced it were one half of them asleep; their work has no personal flavour, but only the tiresome abstraction of minds cut adrift from the promptings of aesthetic emotion. The *Diary* of Pepys is an exception, although it scarcely belongs to the sphere of conscious literary effort; it is informal and private, but none the less a sign that there were some people who could enjoy life with true vivacity, especially when they were too young to remember much about the civil war. The poetry of Dryden is more illustrative of our point; even its magnificent richness and grandeur cannot make up for that which is not there, the vital and personal sympathy that gives a unique and magical beauty to the lyrics of Milton, and pervades all that is best in our lyrical poetry from Spenser to Herrick and Marvell, who remained after 1660 the strange survivals of a departed tranquillity.

For these reasons the student of literature feels more at home in the late Tudor and early Jacobean periods than he can again until, as in Dr Johnson's time, the mass of biographical detail enlivens the literary stage with a new and intimate familiarity. It would be rash, indeed, to assert that the Elizabethans closely resemble our own contemporaries; on the contrary, they combined with their extraordinary art an heroic largeness of thought and action, and a magnificence of gesture which would in these days seem profoundly disconcerting. But they were possessed of a directness and sincerity of expression that must win for them the admiration and sympathy of any age; and this gift of expression was enriched by the accumulated experience of the almost unbroken development of a progressive, virile, and intensely national culture. Moreover, humour, the late-comer and the early-leaver, descended upon this country in the sixteenth century, and worked the magic that she alone can work, making intercourse free and expression natural and unlaboured. But at the first symptoms of civil strife she took fright and fled away, not to return again for a long time, perhaps for a hundred years, and in her absence men had to make the best of wit and fevered hilarity, dismal substitutes. Yet it is important not to over-emphasize the element of social and intellectual disturbance caused in this country by the Reformation before the rise of Puritanism; throughout the Tudor period, and beyond it, advancing culture serenely ignored the disintegrating forces of political and religious unrest; such are the blessings of benevolent and popular despotism.

The sudden destruction of this fertile civilisation is a great obstacle to the historian of English literature, for there is a real breach of continuity. If he embodies the Tudor period in his survey he will arrive at a point where imagination and power of expression are joyfully competitive; but tumultuous catastrophe overwhelmed the entire fabric, and from the general confusion there emerged a literature that sprang from emotional sources entirely alien to the Elizabethan spirit, so different, in fact, that the infectious vigour of the Tudor and early seventeenth century stylists lost for a while its influence. Nor can the Restoration period be regarded merely as an interlude; it introduced new elements into our literature which were destined to be enduring, if not permanent, and among them the element of irony is not the least conspicuous. It is for this reason, as well as to avoid the inconvenience of the breach of continuity just mentioned, that it seemed reasonable to start this historical survey of irony with the Great Rebellion; indeed, from what has gone before it will appear that just those qualities which encouraged irony from Milton onwards were lacking in the former period. Irony thrives when personal animosities are rife; it thrives when particular people, or groups of people, become identified with particular ideas. In short, irony is an engine of controversy and it will be most abundant in a controversial age. The Elizabethan age was not controversial so far as English literature is concerned; it was an age of national outpouring, and consequently its literature is supremely personal, but not in the sense that controversies are personal. People expressed their intimate feelings without imposing themselves upon society as the authors of these confidences; they were not concerned with convicting anyone of error, and they saw no necessity for self-defence; they unburdened their hearts, and there was an end of the matter; one more contribution had been made towards that great and incomparable collection which remains the supreme achievement of our literary art.

With James I the area of controversy increased; more ancient securities became engulfed in the turmoil; but the national literature remained for a while untroubled. The poet's desire for sympathy still triumphed over the intellectual's greed for conquest, and people who could not refrain from shouting had, usually, the good manners to do so in Latin. Irony, indeed, was present in this, as in the Tudor era, but it could hardly yet be called an element of literature; it was confined to a narrow and cultured class where its use was occasional and whimsical, suggestive of much that is best in modern literature. Such irony was tempered by humour and the charity of experience: we have spoken of Dean Colet and Sir Thomas More; from them, as from Robert Burton at this time, that sense of irony which belongs to the academic and philosophical mind was not absent. But criticism remained direct; simple people like Latimer had denounced what they disliked in the roundest terms, and had found the broadest sarcasm quite good enough, when special emphasis seemed necessary; and so it was still; elaborate confutation and finished rhetoric were confined, for the most part, to Latin.

As the political and religious dissensions became more

general, the popular pamphlet encroached upon academic exposition, perhaps to the advantage of both; the pamphlet became more academic, and the thesis less stilted, but increasing bitterness involved both in a wave of scurrility. What is important to our subject is that the spreading inflammation killed the Latin book; England at variance with the continent had need of the universal language, divided against herself she needed her own tongue, and so controversy invaded English literature, and with it the element of irony.

It is true that in the sphere of religion English had been for some time commonly used; the crowning achievement of that literature is Hooker's *Ecclesiastical Polity*, of which the first part was published in 1594. A comparison between Hooker's work and the prose-writings of Milton will illustrate the difference in the prevailing spirit of these two times. Hooker was dealing with the burning question of his day, yet his style is gentle and easy, his expression dignified and restrained. His opinions are exceedingly definite, they might almost be called extreme, yet they are presented with a moderation and a simple directness that makes them surprisingly convincing. There is no bitterness in his writing, no irony, and only the faintest touches of a very mild sarcasm. The people who disagree with him are convicted of inconsistency; when they become very perverse, Hooker becomes so heated as to observe that they 'say nothing at all'; when their obstinacy defeats all attempts at toleration, they are found to be 'most blameworthy in the sight of God, as of man'; and

Hooker has become to posterity as surely 'judicious' as the historian Bede was 'venerable.'

Of a very different nature was Milton, the prose-writer; no one could call him judicious and he was far more terrible than venerable; the gentlest and most melodious of lyrical poets became one of the fiercest and most bitter of English pamphleteers. Milton's life is a caricature of what happened to the nation at large; the fury of his prose has little to do with his subject-matter, which, with the exception of *Areopagitica*, is trivial enough; it is the revenge of his poetical genius blasted by external circumstances. A deep commotion is already evident in *Lycidas*; 'blind mouths,' 'lean and flashy songs' are terrible phrases, prophetic of wrath to come, but few could have guessed what manner of wrath, and what a surprising fulfilment of the promise, 'To-morrow to fresh woods and pastures new.'

In Milton's life the Puritan tragedy was enacted in miniature; the rule of saints resulted in a tyranny be-cause they were in a perpetual minority and weakened by dissensions among themselves. In theory they wanted freedom of conscience and a godly toleration, but the obstinacy of their brethren drove them to coercion; they wanted to love, but innumerable enmities and hatreds employed their time; and in the universal chaos, for which they were in part responsible, they hardened their hearts and condemned their neighbours. In the same way did Milton bring upon himself a querulous and combatant isolation; he had taken up the pen to declare the glory of the new and golden age about to dawn, and to sweep aside the last obstructions of the old order; but violent emotion rent the stifled poet; his ridiculous opinions involved him in antagonisms which blurred the charitable sanity of his fundamental toleration; his magnificent prose was spent in demanding of his opponents 'the rhubarb of restitution and of satisfaction,' and upon these dismal polemics he spent the vigour of his irony. The nature of Milton's irony is true to the circumstances which produced it; it is, on the whole, incomplete and unrestrained, because it lacks the sure foundation of an adequate *casus belli*; and the wrath behind it, being an unreasonable wrath, is always overflowing and disturbing the outward suavity that is essential to successful irony. The following example, albeit it is taken from the *Areopagitica*, is typical of Milton's second-best and most common ironical style. It is very effective and very vigorous, but spoilt in places by an excess of rage.

These are the pretty Responsaries, these are the dear Antiphonies which so bewitched our Prelates and their chaplains with the goodly echo they made; and besotted us to the gay imitation of a lordly Imprimature; one from Lambeth, one from the West end of St Paul's; so apishly Romanizing, that the word of command was still set down in Latin...perhaps, as they thought, because no vulgar tongue was worthy to express the pure conceit of an Imprimature; but rather, as I hope, for that our English, the language of men ever famous and foremost in the achievement of liberty, will not easily find servile letters enow to spell such a dictatory presumption Englisht.

The ironical element is betrayed by fierce expressions

like 'besotted' and 'apishly,' but the passage is, nevertheless, a fine example of irony used with vigour and
versatility, and the sudden conception at the end of the
free exclusiveness of the English language is an exceedingly effective change of front. Yet the personal indignation of the author is, as nearly always with Milton,
far too apparent; the spirit which animated the conclusion of the pamphlet on *Reformation in England*,
placing with unrivalled magnificence of diction the
author's friends 'amidst the Hymns and Hallelujahs of
Saints' and his enemies where they shall be 'the trample
and spurn of all the other damned'—this redundant
vindictiveness nearly always vitiates Milton's irony,
until it is degraded to an extremity of personal invective
in the Latin polemics against Salmasius and 'Morus.'
But what are we to expect from one who had descended
so suddenly from the greatest heights of lyrical experience? Luckily, Milton was a magician (or he would not
have left his poetical elysium) and wherever he went,
he took his magic with him; it does not greatly matter
what he has said, for his speech is in itself supremely
beautiful. With examples of the dreary abuse which
somehow retains an ironical element of sorts, we will
not burden these pages; it is sufficient to say that the
Latin has English equivalents, scattered broadcast
through the prose works. Nor does it seem of any use
to multiply examples of Milton's most typical, hybrid
irony, envisaged in the extract already given: indeed,
one difficulty of this subject, as of many, is that whereas
quotations dragged from their context are both uncon-

vincing and deceptive, this obstacle can only be overcome by extending them to an unbearable length.

Had Milton's subjects been of a less trivial nature, his irony would have assumed a dignity more befitting the grandeur of his prose; as it is, only in the *Areopagitica* are his powers fully displayed. In this work Milton was using precisely the occasion which gives the ironist his chance. In their panic people had forgotten that freedom of speech is the best means of securing moderation of opinion; a vigorous *reductio ad absurdum* was needed to reassert the claims of accepted truth. Milton failed through no lack of ability on his part; the *Areopagitica* must rank with Burke's speeches on the Stamp Act and on Conciliation with America as being one of the most convincing pieces of destructive rhetoric ever produced in English. Milton's irony, however, is in every way superior to Burke's; the latter either tries to be facetious, as in the speech on Economic Reform, and becomes heavy, or he grows exasperated and prejudices the reader against him, as in many passages in the *Letter on the French Revolution*. Between these extremes Milton hits exactly the right note; he remains so grave and logical that his irony has the double effect of being both ludicrous and very sensible. One quotation from the *Areopagitica* must suffice:

If we think to regulate printing, thereby to rectify manners, we must regulate all recreations and pastimes, all that is delightful to man. No music must be heard, no song be set or sung, but what is grave and Doric. There must be licensing dancers, that no gesture, motion, or deportment be taught our Youth, but what by their allowance be thought honest; for such Plato was provided of; It will ask more than the work of twenty licensers to examine all the lutes, violins and guitars in every house; they must not be allowed to prattle as they do, but must be licensed what they may say. And who shall silence all the airs and madrigals, that whisper softness in chambers? The windows also, and the balconies must be thought on; there are shrewd books with dangerous frontispieces set to sale; and who shall prohibit them, shall twenty licensers? The villages, also, must have their visitors to enquire what lectures the bag-pipe and the rebbeck reads even to the Ballantry, and the gamut of every municipal fiddler, for these are the countryman's 'Arcadia' and his 'Monte Mayors.' Next, what more national corruption, for which England hears ill abroad, than household gluttony; who shall be the rectors of our daily rioting?

There is an almost regal liberality in the courtly manner with which Milton lends his imagination to illuminate the idea of his opponents; there is a 'give and take' about it which is very amiable—and very convincing; and all the time, the real Milton, angry and derisive, is hidden away behind the stateliness of his prose, while the absurd fatuities flow smoothly and contentedly on. The only danger is that in their satisfaction they may flow too long, and incite in us an intolerance of the bitterly complacent author. A sense of humour will teach the ironist to be tactful, but Milton was too colossal for humour.

It is, at any rate, time that we left him. In an age of feeble and irritable ironists he stands a gigantic figure, alone worth our consideration: his worst irony can compete with any of his contemporaries' maledictions as an exhibition of sheer ill-temper and a wretched, bullying spirit; his best irony, on the other hand, stands by itself in attaining to a dignity, and almost to a grandeur, very rarely associated with ironical utterance, and as an appeal to common-sense and a wide and sane toleration it has not been surpassed. The pity is that there is so little of it.

Milton was exceptional rather than typical, but we do not intend to trouble the reader with examples of the typical, for it is dreary and contemptible. A short exploration into the innumerable pamphlets, political and religious, which abounded in those days will very soon satisfy the curiosity of anybody in this respect. It will be sufficient to point out that the Restoration did not immediately improve matters; the particular annoyance of being regarded as an enemy of society was transferred from one type of person to another; the religions which formerly had exulted in their emancipation now exulted in their martyrdom, and *vice versa*, and both kinds of exultation were unpleasant. In short, there survived between the various classes of Englishmen just the same hatreds that had existed before, and in some cases they grew worse; at any rate the same peevish irony continued to pass between them. Let us pass on to more cheerful considerations.

CHAPTER III
JONATHAN SWIFT

If, in the beginning, irony was born in an age of controversy and became the tool of private faction, let us not contend that in all cases it has sprung from the deep commotions of personal resentment or conscious pugnacity. We have already shown how fundamental we believe the connection between irony and these dreary passions to be, but we have also shown how Milton broke away from them in the *Areopagitica*, and found in irony a very potent weapon for the destruction of prevailing error rather than individual folly. After Milton irony fell back again into the dismal bickerings of indignant and conceited men; even *Hudibras* did not improve matters much. It is true that Butler aimed his satire at a type rather than an individual, but the general attitude of his attack is depressingly vindictive. He wrote at the height of the Anglican exultation and was simply pandering to the spirit of his time. Where his satire becomes intensified into irony, we feel the remembrance of private indignation, or an eager desire to make the most of some popular fancy, to rub in still further the rude sting of some hackneyed taunt. The great merit of Butler consists in the fact that he was a poet, in his common-sense, and in a certain quaint and vivid manner of expression that he made his own. When he passes from satire to irony, it is nearly always because his temper has got the better of him, and it is seldom because he wishes to dispose of some absurd conceit by intellectual ridicule, which is the proper use of irony.

Henceforth, it will largely be the purpose of this essay to show how the authors of more modern times have, by slow degrees, done much to rescue irony from the bitterness and loss of temper in which it became engulfed, to show how they elevated it, until it became the devoted, yet tempestuous, servant of that Comic Spirit whose unerring powers of criticism Meredith has depicted so vigorously and so well, and in their hands exchanged derision for a gentler form of mocking. Irony, thus emancipated, became ambitious: she suffered the restraints of polite society that she might enter the highest places, and ventured within the charitable, yet exclusive, domain of humour; and in these quiet regions Irony found a champion in someone almost as much an intruder, as she was herself.

Jonathan Swift was a man in a perpetual temper; he hated and he denounced with a fury that dominated his life. He did worse than this; he slandered people in a furtive and secretive fashion, and struck at them from behind. Yet Swift has been tragically misunderstood by posterity, and it is partly his own fault; his savagery is so surprising that we forget the contemptible nature of his victims; we think of him as wildly ill-tempered, scolding indiscriminately whatsoever provoked his wrath; and it is not true. Swift's character was complex; more than anything he was an artist, and he possessed the distinctive charity of art. He denounced nothing that was misguided and also generous; error arising from genuine ignorance escaped his avenging irony;

but he hated all forms of humbug and obstinate conceit, and he lived in an age when these things were very abundant. He detested meanness and he was surrounded by it; every kind of intellectual dishonesty was rife in his time, and he disliked it very heartily. No doubt he was over-ambitious, and his manners were not of the best, but both Dr Johnson and Thackeray are wrong when they imply that there is something rather shady about Swift, that he is not quite honest, that he would tell you one thing and contradict it behind your back. He was very honest, and desperately sincere, but he would not parade the fact any more than he did his extensive and secret generosity in gifts of money; at any rate, and it is more to our purpose, he used his irony only against what was despicable and unpardonably absurd, and when he lost his temper and ran to personalities and unpleasant slander, it would be difficult to prove that the wretched victim did not deserve it. We will let him speak for himself:

> His vein, ironically grave,
> Exposed the fool and lashed the knave...
> Perhaps I may allow the Dean
> Had too much satire in his vein,
> And seemed determined not to starve it
> Because no age could more deserve it.
> Yet malice never was his aim,
> He lashed the vice but spared the name;
> No individual could resent,
> Where thousands equally were meant.
> His satire points at no defect
> But what all mortals may correct:

> For he abhorred that senseless tribe
> Who call it humour when they gibe:
> He spared a hump, or crooked nose,
> Whose owners set not up for beaux.
> True genuine dulness moved his pity,
> Unless it offer'd to be witty;
> Those who their ignorance confest
> He ne'er offended with a jest.

And as for the superior people all around him, he says
with characteristic irony:

> Great folks are of a finer mould;
> Lord, how politely they can scold!

We believe the poet's estimate of himself, quoted above,
to be very fair and just. His place in English irony is
not only a great one, he reigns supreme; intensely
individualistic, and successfully imitated by no one, he
nevertheless set the note that dominated English satire
until it was superseded by the novel, and he not only
established irony in its place as the 'humour of satire,'
but he pointed the way in *Gulliver's Travels* to those who
at a later period employed it so effectively in their
novels, although in this region his influence is less para-
mount. That Swift was conscious and, indeed, jealous
of his place as an ironist appears in the following lines:

> I grieve to be outdone by Gay
> In my own humorous biting way;
> Arbuthnot is no more my friend
> Who dares to irony pretend,
> Which I was born to introduce,
> Refined it first, and show'd its use.

It will be impossible to speak adequately about Swift as the father of English irony, unless we allow ourselves a brief digression to consider the position that satire came to take in English literature after the Restoration. The potentialities of irony, as displayed by Milton, were perceived by no one, and on his death, it was dragged back, as we have said, to the sordid regions of personal wranglings. In this dreary sense the Restoration period went far to outbid the Great Rebellion itself as an age of irony, but it also deserves the name in another and a better sense. Congreve, Gay, and Sheridan have, in their different ways, shown that comedy is not without its hold upon this country, but they have shown also how slender that hold is, and within what narrow limits comedy itself has been here confined. The Comic Spirit is all-pervading; she visits every sphere of human experience, that she may laugh out of countenance all that is ridiculous, stilted, or insincere; and of this universal scrutiny comedy should be the literary expression. In France, indeed, she has been so, but in England only that which is more superficial in society, the fleeting topics of the fashion, have suffered her judgment in comedy: the more general and abiding themes of human life, those permanent or recurring weaknesses that can be found with unfailing regularity in any civilisation, have in this country been made the themes of satire, a form of expression far less suited than comedy to the gentle criticism of the Comic Spirit. The limitations of satire gave irony its chance, for here at any rate the Comic Spirit could indulge in those flights of the imagination, to which she is so prone, and which she finds so essential; thus irony became, so to speak, her chief of staff, and yet always retained a kind of bitterness that remained an uncertain and disquieting factor. The novel finally remedied the deficiencies that the Englishman's distaste for comedy had caused, but until this time irony supplied, as best she could, the only means whereby the authors of a finer criticism, too subtle for the blunt caricature of satire, achieved a somewhat precarious freedom.

This projection of irony into an accepted type of literary criticism is an ingenious and characteristic achievement of the English, making the Restoration period and the early eighteenth century deserve, as we have said, in a better sense, to be called the Age of Irony. It is easy to feel how unsuited were the people of that time to the more delicate understanding of comedy, but difficult to find a really satisfactory reason. If we say that a good sense of comedy demands a sense of humour, which these men had not, mistaking it for their heartless wit, it can be answered that the ironist must likewise have a sense of humour. And it is very true that Swift has given abundant proof in the *Journal of Stella* that his piercing imagination could be softened by genuine humour; Arbuthnot, also, second only to Swift as an ironist, has a certain whimsicality about his writings that betrays very forcibly the humour which led all who knew him to testify to the remarkable charm of his personality. The fact is that these great ironists of an ironical age had just those qualities that their contemporaries lacked; that is why they were never successfully imitated, and yet so great was their influence that they gave to their age its predominant tone. Swift and Arbuthnot chose irony because it was the vehicle of expression most congenial to their hearers, and so the question as to why ironical utterance was so particularly the product of those times is still unanswered; the characters of Swift and Arbuthnot will tell us nothing; they were the exceptions of their age, and they became its consummation only because genius is as adaptable as it is compelling.

Matthew Prior, a satirist of considerable merit, but lacking perhaps the detachment and the imagination of the true ironist, described very faithfully, albeit unconsciously, the spirit of his times in a poem on Pleasure:

> Sadly, O reason, is thy power express'd,
> Thou gloomy tyrant of the frighted breast!
>
> .   .   .   .   .
>
> But do I call thee tyrant or complain,
> How hard thy laws, how absolute thy reign?
> While thou, alas! art but an empty name,
> To no two men, who e'er discoursed, the same.

These rather pompous lines contain the explanation of much that is most conspicuous in those curious people: the great Age of Reason was, not unnaturally, an age of scepticism. The great thing was not to find out what was true, but to discover and confute what was false; the men who made the intellectual boast that all truth would be disclosed in time by empirical methods were none the less pessimists at heart. Their hatred of enthusiasm must not be confused with the mid-eighteenth century attitude of comfortable moderation; it was a far more cynical affair, it sprang from the disillusionment that still assailed people in the long reaction from nearly a century of religious strife. Thus it was that to them a downright exposure of folly seemed about the best thing a man could hope to achieve; to such a frame of mind comedy will make no appeal; for although the Comic Spirit is the arch-eradicator of folly, she does so in the joyful confidence of the support of positive truth and appeals to the positive wisdom of mankind. Satire and irony also make their appeal to common sense. Truth remains the final arbiter, but their lasting aim and object is a great negation, *reductio ad absurdum*; they will not turn from vanquished folly to point with the Comic Spirit the happy contrast of good sense. What is that to do with them? They were just the happy couple that our strange worshippers of 'sad Reason' wanted; there was no danger from them of an appeal to the heart, a thing so disagreeable and discomforting.

In such an atmosphere, a man of Swift's temperament and genius could scarcely fail to make his mark; he had exactly those powers of logical extension that must appeal to any society professing to admire Reason above all things. But he had, in addition, a gift which does not always accompany rational ability, the imagination to choose with triumphant effect the premises upon which the logical fabric shall be erected; he had a most piercing insight into human nature; he had no philosophy, except the negative kind, which consists in an intense dislike of all humbug. He could thus pursue an absurd conceit with remorseless logic to its utter and swift destruction; no subject presented any difficulty to his Irish fluency and insatiability; he could talk with apparent earnestness on any subject, not excluding *A Modest Proposal for Preventing the Children of Poor People in Ireland from being a Burden to their Parents or Country*, i.e. cannibalism. Burning with secret indignation at the social distress of his country, he presents his scheme with complete suavity and business-like persuasion. 'We can incur no danger of disobliging England. For this kind of commodity will not bear exportation, the flesh being of too tender a consistence to admit of long continuance in salt; although perhaps I could name a country which would be glad to eat up a whole nation without it.' And from whence did the idea come into Swift's head? It sprang from a consideration of the maxim that the 'People are the riches of a nation,' a maxim tragically unsuited for the Ireland of his day. When to this extraordinary power of detachment was added a lively consciousness of his own genius, great ambition, and an equally great contempt for the inferior people who thwarted it, we have indeed the makings of a super-ironist.

So important a position does Swift hold in English irony that we may, perhaps, be excused for the number and extent of the following quotations. Irony can be put to many uses by methods equally various, but there is hardly a use or method of which Swift will not furnish an example, and in many cases the best to be found: for this reason it seemed wise to confine ourselves to his works in illustrating the irony of his period, rather than, for variety's sake, to draw our examples from a number of inferior men.

One great merit of Swift's irony is that it is so often double-edged; he attacks general tendencies through particular absurdities, and *vice versa*; he is continually allusive, thereby giving a kind of lambency to much that would fall rather flat as a sustained, but merely general, denouncement. It is very hard to achieve success in continued irony, but Swift achieves it. The following extract from *The Tale of a Tub* is, to use an ugly expression, a multiplex assault. The main objective is the arrogance and insufficiency of authors, but he combines this with an attack on the length and dreariness of the fashionable preface, and, in the process, has a dig at Dryden. Nor do critics, wits, and even the innocent general reader escape unscathed.

... Such exactly is the fate, at this time, of Prefaces, Epistles, Advertisements, Introductions, Prolegomenas, Apparatus's, To the Readers. This expedient was admirable at first; our great Dryden has long carried it as far as it would go, and with incredible success. He has often told me in confidence that the world would never have suspected him to be so great a poet, if he had not assured them so frequently in his prefaces, that it was impossible they could either doubt or forget it. Perhaps it may be so; however, I much fear his instructions have edify'd out of their place, and taught men to grow wiser in certain points, where he never intended they should; for it is lamentable to observe with what a lazy scorn many of the yawning readers of our age, do now-a-days twirl over fourty or fifty pages of preface or dedication (which is the usual modern stint) as if it were so much Latin. Tho' it must be also allow'd on the other hand that a very considerable number is known to proceed criticks and wits, by reading nothing else. Into which factions I think all present readers may be justly divided. Now, for myself, I profess to be one of the former sort; and therefore having the modern inclination to expatiate upon the beauty of my own productions, and display the bright parts of my discourse, I thought it best to do it in the body of the work, where, as it now lies, it makes a very considerable addition to the bulk of the volume, *a circumstance by no means to be neglected by a skilful writer.*

Having thus paid my due deference and acknowledgment to an established custom of our newest authors, by a long digression unsought for, and an universal censure unprovoked; by forcing into light, with much pains and dexterity, my own excellencies and other men's defaults, with great justice to myself and candour to them; I now happily resume my Subject, to the infinite satisfaction, both of the Reader and the Author.

This is a strange mixture of satire and irony, and a certain whimsicality which is not quite humour; and it is very wide in its embrace, so wide, in fact, that we feel slightly injured by it ourselves; at any rate, the italics are Swift's and not ours. Sometimes Swift mingles with his irony a very direct form of criticism; the following reflections upon the age which produced Titus Oates and Dr Sacheverell have a conclusion that might almost be called violent:

The bulk of the people consist, in a manner, wholly of discoverers, witnesses, informers, accusers, prosecutors,

37

evidences, swearers, together with their several subservient and subaltern instruments, all under the colours, the conduct, and pay of ministers of state and their deputies. The plots in that kingdom are usually the workmanship of those persons, who desire to raise their own characters of profound politicians; to restore new vigour to the administration; to stifle or divert popular discontents; to fill their pockets with forfeitures; and raise or sink the public credit, as either shall best answer their private advantage. It is first agreed and settled among them what persons shall be accused of a plot; then effectual care is taken to secure all their letters and papers, and put the criminals in chains. These papers are delivered to a set of artists, very dexterous in finding out the mysterious meanings of words, syllables, and letters: for instance, they can discover a flock of geese to signify a senate; a lame dog, an invader; the plague, a standing army; a buzzard, a prime minister; the goat, a high priest; a gibbet, a secretary of state; a sieve, a court lady; a broom, a revolution; a mouse-trap, an employment; a bottomless pit, a treasury; a sink, a court; a cat and bells, a favourite; a broken reed, a court of justice; an empty tun, a general; a running sore, the administration. (*Gulliver's Travels.*)

Equally to the point, and no less bitter, although less savage, is the next extract, which gains in ironical effect by being put into the mouth of the King of Brobdingnag in the form of several questions, which are tactfully left unanswered. This device of making the most trenchant observations occur, as it were, casually, and quite ingenuously, is a favourite trick of Swift's. In the present instance he profits by being in the position of a novelist and having a free hand to arrange his own dramatic setting: in this way the most vigorous condemnation can be made polite and superficially innocuous by the careful fostering of a complete sense of ingenuousness. Gulliver had been telling the King about our parliamentary institutions; and his Majesty

then desired to know what arts were practised in electing those whom I called commoners: whether a stranger, with a strong purse, might not influence the vulgar voters to choose him before their landlord, or the most considerable gentleman in the neighbourhood. How it came to pass that people were so violently bent upon getting into this assembly, which I allowed to be a great trouble and expense, often to the ruin of their families, without any salaries or pension: because that appeared such an exalted strain of virtue that his Majesty seemed to doubt it might possibly not be always sincere: and he desired to know whether such zealous gentlemen could have any views of refunding themselves for the charges and trouble they were at by sacrificing the public good. . .in conjunction with a corrupted ministry.

This kind of thing came quite naturally to Swift; sometimes he maintains the style for a considerable time, and, curiously enough, he does not grow dull as other people would; there is about him a triumphant insolence that is, somehow, very witty, and he is always so gloriously in the right. But his bitterness is at times exceedingly great. The predominant influence in his life may or may not have been personal ambition (not, as we think); but there can then be no doubt that, if it was not, Swift's great object in life was the furtherance of the established Church, and in writing of Church affairs his irony is keenest. The secession of the nonjurors had robbed the Church of much of its vitality,

39

and lay opinion was sceptical and lazy. How shall we revive it? Obviously we must make it fashionable, is Swift's acid answer in *A Project for the Advancement of Religion*, and this must be done by the power of the administration. What follows is taken from *A Letter to a Friend concerning the Mechanical Operation of the Spirit* and seems to us the last word in bitterness; it is also a good example of the elaborate display of logical paraphernalia that Swift introduces to heighten the effect of mock ingenuousness whenever he is about to pursue a particularly significant topic. He has been talking about 'enthusiasm' and continues:

The word in its universal application may be defined, a lifting up of the soul or its faculties above matter. This description will hold good in general, but I am only to understand it as applied to religion, wherein there are three ways of ejaculating the soul, or transporting it beyond the sphere of matter. The first is the immediate act of God, and is called 'prophecy' or 'inspiration.' The second is the immediate act of the Devil and is called 'possession.' The third is the product of natural causes, the effect of strong imagination, and is called 'spleen,' 'violent anger,' 'fear,' 'grief,' 'pain,' and the like. These have been abundantly treated on by Authors, and therefore, shall not employ my enquiry. But, the fourth method of religious enthusiasm, or launching out of the soul, as it is purely an effect of artifice and mechanick operation, has been sparingly handled, or not at all, by any writer; because though it is an act of great antiquity, yet having been confined to few persons, it long wanted those advancements and refinements, which it afterwards met with, since it is grown so epidemick, and fallen into so many cultivating hands.

It is therefore upon this Mechanical Operation of the Spirit that I mean to treat, as it is at present performed by our British workmen. . . .

And so, on the wings of his imagination, Swift pursues relentlessly the wild career of his dismal investigation, and, as though he were the Ancient Mariner, follow him we must, while he drags us along with him through all the slums of the human mind. At his approach all disguises fall away; he is the avenging spirit; the naked strength of irony is in him, and he has used it in the service of Truth. We may follow with indignation, but not at him should we direct our anger, for he is always right, and this, as he has himself pointed out, is not so wicked as is commonly supposed.

The inanimate objects of everyday life would not leave the Dean in peace; he saw sermons in everything, and monstrous similitudes were always arising in his mind.

I conceive, as to the business of being profound, that it is with writers as with wells; a person with good eyes may see to the bottom of the deepest, provided any water be there; and that often, when there is nothing in the world at the bottom besides dryness and dirt, though it be but a yard and a half under ground, it shall pass, however, for wondrous deep upon no wiser a reason than because it is wondrous dark.

Swift could not escape from himself any more than his unfortunate victims.

We will take our leave of Swift in a happier vein. The last book of *Gulliver's Travels*, the voyage to the country of the Houyhnhnms is, perhaps, one of the most successful indictments ever drawn up by a man against the human race. Swift conceived a country where horses were endowed with great intelligence and all good qualities, and only man was vile. With great cunning, he endowed the Houyhnhnms with just those admirable qualities most conspicuously absent in his time; they were so tolerant, and quiet; so courtly and self-contained; in short, they had all the endowments of good-breeding and self-control. Man, on the other hand, as envisaged in the Yahoos, was bestial to a degree, and yet he remained terribly human; he was noisy and quarrelsome, avaricious, and self-centred, not to mention his laziness and general slovenliness. With great skill Swift avoids overstressing these points; he lets the situation read its own lesson; he simply follows out his original conception with great vivacity and, perhaps, a little too graphically. But the arch-ironist is indulging his imagination to its fullest extent, and he will not spoil the effect by an excess of bitterness. Parts of the fourth book are terrible enough, but for the most part Swift's artistic sense is triumphant, and the whole is an ironical achievement of the very first rank. We shall content ourselves with one quotation. It is chosen not for its ironical quality, but as an example of Swift's extraordinary power of following his imagination, and his perfect gravity and restraint in no matter how ludicrous a situation; and finally because it represents his style in English prose at its very best.

When all was ready, and the day came for my departure, I took leave of my master and lady, and the whole family, my eyes flowing with tears, and my heart quite sunk with grief. But his honour, out of curiosity, and perhaps (if I may speak it without vanity) partly out of kindness, was determined to see me in my canoe; and got several of his neighbouring friends to accompany him. I was forced to wait above an hour for the tide, and then observing the wind very fortunately bearing towards the island to which I intended to steer my course, I took a second leave of my master: but as I was going to prostrate myself to kiss his hoof, he did me the honour to raise it gently to my mouth.

I am not ignorant how much I have been censured for mentioning this last particular. For my detractors are pleased to think it improbable that so illustrious a person should descend to give so great a mark of distinction to so inferior a person as I. Neither have I forgot how apt some travellers are to boast of extraordinary favours they have received. But if these censurers were better acquainted with the noble and courteous nature of the Houyhnhnms, they would soon change their opinion.

Swift established irony in a place in English literature to which Milton could only at times carry it. Henceforth it was the duty of irony to keep guard over public opinion, to preserve a common sense of fairness in all particulars, to recall men to a mental equilibrium endangered by the allurements of intellectual fashion. With error arising from ignorance, or a slowness to observe the ridiculous, the Comic Spirit can deal, but there are times when she needs the assistance of irony's sterner and harsher methods; such methods are necessary to dispel the obstinate illusions arising from intellectual pride, for they are very contagious, and such opinions as come from intellectual dishonesty or mere laziness, in the innumerable cases where the wish is father to the thought.

All this Swift understood; his only fault was an excess of zeal, and an inability to curb sufficiently his swelling indignations; and his irony suffers for it, for it is often wanting in dignity. We will leave the Dean with a final quotation from the poem upon his own death which he wrote at a time when his ambition was finally quelled by the certainty that he would never climb higher than the Deanery of St Patrick's, and when he felt the slow encroachment of madness already coming upon him.

> He gave what little wealth he had
> To build a house for fools and mad;
> And showed by one satiric touch
> No nation wanted it so much
> That kingdom he has left his debtor;
> I hope it soon may have a better.

At times, when the violence of Swift's abuse shakes our confidence in him, when his lapses into coarseness seem intolerable, we should remember how great a hero he was to the common people of Dublin, and how large and extensive was his charity; and these considerations may lead us to see in Swift himself the curious and anomalous position of irony in English literature at that time.

CHAPTER IV

SWIFT'S CONTEMPORARIES

DANIEL DEFOE AND DR ARBUTHNOT

Despite the greatness of Swift's place in the history of irony, it would not be just to his contemporaries to forget them altogether. Overshadowed they are, completely; in the ironic field they have essayed nothing that the Dean has not also achieved with greater success than they. But two of them at any rate must be briefly considered here, not for any outstanding originality or pioneer work in the history of our subject, but because, while doing nothing that Swift does not do also, they have shifted a little the focus of ironic endeavour by a difference of temperament rather than of topic or technique. These two men are Dr Arbuthnot and Daniel Defoe. They are as unlike each other as they are respectively unlike Swift. Both of them are quite free from the deep unrest which never left the Dean's mind; his bitterness is not theirs, and happiness, with all its restfulness, does not seem to have eluded them as it did the Irishman's excited spirit. Defoe was constitutionally happy, and Arbuthnot was constitutionally calm. The latter was, indeed, an embodiment of refinement for his age. Speaking of 'the eminent writers of Queen Anne's reign,' Dr Johnson said, 'I think Dr Arbuthnot the first man among them. He was the most universal genius, being an excellent physician, a man of deep learning, and a man of much humour.' Of Defoe, Boswell tells us that Johnson 'allowed a considerable

45

share of merit to a man, who, bred as a tradesman, had written so variously and so well.' There is a suggestion of snobbishness here, but the distinction is a true one. If we would find refinement in Defoe we must look not so much to his breeding as to the many attractive qualities of his character. Arbuthnot was a man of intellectual aloofness and an independent mind. His opinion of the people of his age was not flattering, and he escaped cynicism only by the kindness of his heart. Defoe was second to Pepys alone in his general enjoyment of life and interest in all its aspects; he was everywhere exuberant, in his appreciation, his benignity, and his mockery. From such a temperament we should hardly expect much irony and, indeed, Defoe's irony is seldom 'the exceeding bitter cry' that comes from the prophet in distress, still less is it a high and penetrating dissection of human nature, such as Gibbon produces from his lonely pinnacle. But Defoe lived in an age when irony was expected of authors dealing with current topics. The pamphleteer, the political writer, who ignored this accepted form of polemic would, besides displaying an almost perverse independence, find it difficult to satisfy a society which demanded plain-speaking and ridicule of a very pointed kind.

Defoe was not unwilling to do what was expected of him in this respect: if he lacked the temperament of the true ironist, he possessed qualities which were perhaps more acceptable to the average man about him. Embracing irony as a necessary and established form, he added to it an admirable sense of humour, enlivened by an almost roguish persistence. He would, or could, not be silent when anything provoked his derision or his disapproval. His irony is far too precipitate to be made the vehicle of pent-up emotion or compressed malevolence; on the other hand, it lacks the sense of unemotional detachment, often so effective in irony. Here, as in everything else to do with Defoe, 'cheerfulness was always breaking in,' and if not cheerfulness, some other disturbance equally disruptive of irony, a new idea, or the sudden accession of enthusiasm for what things ought to be like, even if they are not, and a feeling that people are good-hearted enough at bottom, but suffer from a lack of imagination; they cannot envisage things, and the simplicity of Utopia eludes them. There is a passage in *A Journal of the Plague Year* that starts with a suggestion of irony, when it is remembered that Defoe was an enthusiastic, although a tolerant, dissenter, but very quickly the idea of what ought to be dominates his mind, and any idea of irony is forgotten in a generous appeal.

The Dissenters who with uncommon prejudice had broken off from the communion of the Church of England, were now content to come to their parish churches, and to conform to the worship which they did not approve of before; but as the terror of the infection abated, those things all returned again to their less desirable channel, and to the course they were in before.

I mention this but historically, I have no mind to enter into arguments to move either or both sides to a more charitable compliance one with another. . . . But this I may repeat again, that it is evident death will reconcile us all: on the other side of the grave we shall be all brethren again;

47

in heaven, whither I hope we may come from all parties and persuasions, we shall find neither prejudice nor scruple; there we shall be of one principle and of one opinion. Why we cannot be content to go hand in hand to the place where we shall join hand in hand without the least hesitation, and with the most complete harmony and affection; I say, why we cannot do so here I can say nothing to, neither shall I say anything more of it, but that it remains to be lamented.

This is typical of all Defoe's work; strong feeling invariably leads him to the most simple and direct forms of utterance, where it would have driven Swift to the bitterest of irony.

Now and again, however, Defoe maintained a formal irony throughout a work dealing with a subject about which he felt deeply. Such cases, as might be expected, belong to that section of his writings which reveal him as the pamphleteer so typical of his age. *The Shortest way with Dissenters* is one of the best known of his pamphlets. In this the ironical vein is continuous throughout, but, considering the subject and Defoe's own sentiments, it is irony of a singularly unprovocative nature. He is content to ridicule his opponents by gravely enunciating the preposterous in their name and supports High Anglicanism with a fervent and a fevered logic. His self-control had its reward and its punishment; the reward was that some eager churchmen praised God for their new champion, and the punishment that Defoe went to the pillory and from thence to Newgate when the truth came out. Certainly he credited the Anglicans with a gift of righteous indigna-

tion. 'The more numerous (the Dissenters), the more
dangerous, and therefore the more need to suppress
them; *and God has suffered us to bear them as goads in our
sides, for not utterly extinguishing them long ago.*' The Dissenters the mock Anglican harangued as follows:

Gentlemen, the time of mercy is past, your day of Grace is
over; you should have practised peace, and moderation,
and charity, if you expected any yourselves. We have heard
none of this lesson for fourteen years past. [Defoe is writing
in 1702.] We have been huffed and bullied with your Act
of Toleration; you have told us that you are the Church
established by law, as well as others; have set up your
canting synagogues at our church doors, and the church and
members have been loaded with reproaches, with oaths,
with abjurations, and what not; where has been the mercy,
the forbearance, the charity, you have shown to tender
consciences of the Church of England, that could not take
oaths as fast as you made them; that having sworn allegiance
to their lawful and rightful King, could not dispense with
that oath, their King being still alive, and swear to your new
hodge-podge of a Dutch government? These have been
turned out of their livings, and they and their families left
to starve; their estates double taxed, to carry on a war they
had no hand in, and you got nothing by. What account
can you give of the multitudes you have forced to comply,
against their consciences, with your new sophistical politics,
who, like new converts in France, sin because they can't
starve? And now the tables are turned upon you, you must
not be persecuted, 'tis not a Christian spirit.

Even a small knowledge of the history of the times will
make this remarkable pamphlet very enjoyable reading:
nowhere is Defoe's vivacity and elasticity of mind more

apparent. Amidst many of the old battle-cries that had worn out an entire generation, he introduced some very telling arguments in favour of the Church's case, so certain, we must suppose, he felt of the righteousness of the cause of the Dissenters. And yet, even in his most polemical writings, this certainty of the rightness of one side is never convincing; it is there superficially, but it wears the appearance of something heartily adopted. The real Defoe is behind this insecure mask, a man not aloof from his neighbours, swayed by the same passions, and enlivened by the same interests as they, but possessing a keener sense of perspective and a more clearly defined morality, whereby he escapes the artificial congruities that result from the organisation and conflict of parties.

In such a manner Defoe preserved his liberty, and it was a liberty of sympathy rather than an unfettered right of criticism that he demanded. He can criticise with fervour at times, as, for instance, he criticises the *True-born Englishman* of mixed descent who reviled his King (William III) as a foreigner, and 'sought his aid, and then his part forsakes.' But his irony is, on the whole, an indulgent irony; remarkably indulgent, indeed, for the age in which he lived. With his intense interest in every problem of human life, Defoe combined a shrewdness, a versatility, and a buoyancy of spirit that gave an unusual vivacity to all he wrote. With these properties it was inevitable that he should constantly ridicule and frequently upbraid his contemporaries. But he is far too interested in everybody and everything to bear malice or feel a lasting contempt, and the fact that his irony betrays no lack of generosity, or fundamental bitterness, is the measure of the service that he did to the topical literature of his age.

The amount that he wrote is immense. His works of fiction are well known, as also are *A Journal of the Plague Year* and the *History of the Union*. Amongst a host of shorter publications, *The Political History of the Devil* is perhaps the richest in mild irony and satire, while by far the most amusing of his definitely ironical works is a short pamphlet entitled, *What if the Pretender should come?* It is a significant thing that Defoe's irony was often misunderstood in those extravagant times, and this pamphlet cost him some days in prison until its true import had sunk in and brought him release.

'It has been the disaster of all parties in this nation,' he wrote, 'to be very hot in their turn, and as often as they have been so, I have differed with them all and shall do so. . . . To attain at the happy calm, which is the consideration that should move us all (and he would merit to be called the nation's physician who could prescribe the specific for it), I think I may be allowed to say a conquest of parties will never do it—a balance of parties may.'

This is more than Defoe's political creed, it is the creed of his whole life. He wrote a pamphlet entitled *Everybody's business is nobody's business*, and made everybody's business his own; but the equable person with a power of ridicule who enters every dispute, in an ill-tempered age, preaching moderation and proportion, will not be welcomed as a peacemaker nor accounted a wise man, and this Defoe found out. But his unquenchable loquacity and a genuine desire to help people caused him to persevere; and after all, if politics become too hot for a time, one can write a *Plan of the English Commerce* or *Trade and Navigation considered*, and then, if one should have the misfortune to offend the merchants, there is still the *Unsufferable Behaviour of Servants*, a topic upon which all will be agreed; and for a large and profitable sale there can surely be nothing so good as the *Uses and Abuses of the Marriage Bed*.

Arbuthnot, on the other hand, made nobody's business his own. It is true that his satire dealt with current topics, but he never in any way identified himself with public movements. Thus his Toryism consisted only in a greater readiness to deride the opposite side, but it did not secure the Tories from derision of any kind. He was, in short, a recluse, a man of a kind and critical mind. A learned physician and an excellent mathematician, he despised and condemned the age in which he lived, but to his friends he showed a great capacity for affection and a singularly lovable disposition, to which they all bear witness. Arbuthnot was physician to the Queen, and we cannot refrain from quoting some of the letter he wrote to Swift on her death; it is so typical of the gentle philosopher who thought himself so much more misanthropical than he really was.

August 12, 1714.

My dear Friend,

I thank you for your kind letter, which is very comfortable upon such a melancholy occasion. My dear Mistress's days were numbered even in my imagination, and could not exceed such certain limits, but of that smaller number a great deal was cut off by the last troublesome scene among her servants. I believe sleep was never more welcome to a weary traveller than death was to her. . . .

I have an opportunity calmly and philosophically to consider that treasure of vileness and baseness, that I always believed to be in the heart of man; and to behold them exert their insolence and baseness: every new instance, instead of surprising and grieving me, as it does some of my friends, really diverts me and in a manner improves my theory: though I think I have not met with it in my own case, except from one man, and he was very much mistaken, for to him I would not abate one grain of my proud spirit. . . .

I am sure I can never forget you, till I meet with (what is impossible) another, whose conversation I can delight in so much as in Dr Swift's: and yet that is the smallest thing I ought to value you for. That hearty sincere friendship, that plain and open ingenuity in all your commerce, is what I am sure I never can find in another man. I shall want often a faithful monitor, one that would vindicate me behind my back, and tell me my faults to my face. God knows I write this with tears in my eyes. . . .

With Arbuthnot we may most suitably take our leave of the old order, for there is much about him which points to the new. This attractive writer, who found his compatriots so distasteful, nevertheless understood so well their fundamental characteristics that John Bull, the generic title of Englishmen, is taken from a creation of his pen. In *Law is a Bottomless Pit* which, with various extensions, became *The History of John Bull*, Arbuthnot's

53

methods and personality can be clearly perceived. His mind was possessed of a peculiar ingenuity, and he and Swift together indulged in many pleasant and rather childish fancies, but whereas the more impetuous Swift had a liking for practical jokes, Arbuthnot preferred conundrums and riddles. He stands for much that was best in the lighter productions of the Age of Wit, for he added to it a generosity of the heart unusual in his day.

The History of John Bull is ingenious in the extreme; the various persons in the history represent the several powers engaged in the war of the Spanish Succession, in whom national characteristics, or, as in the case of France, an absolute monarchy, the characteristics of kings, are ably portrayed; and a long and exasperating lawsuit follows very faithfully the course of the war. Arbuthnot succeeds admirably in exposing the social evils which made it possible for a dynastic dispute to result in so much misery, and he did not spare the general dishonesty upon which diplomacy is built. But the work, while being a satire upon European politics, is especially convincing as a satire upon England and English behaviour during the war. We, however, are concerned with irony, and in this respect Arbuthnot's claim upon our consideration lies not so much in what he did, as in what he omitted to do. In the sense in which Swift was an ironist, Arbuthnot certainly did no more than 'to irony pretend.' He had none of that passion which pursued the Dean, and he had no desire to make irony the scourge that Swift made it. By far the most telling parts of *John Bull* are not so much ironical as rather bitterly satirical, and of this the chapter where Jack (the Calvinists) hangs himself is a good example. There is no real duplicity of meaning apart from the substitution of false names, and of people for countries. Arbuthnot's irony is occasional and very brilliant; and where it appears, it does not always betoken, as one would expect, a gust of emotion so much as a sudden accession of wit. It is true that in such cases the wit is aimed, as a rule, at something contemptible enough, but one feels that the irony is added to it, not so much out of bitterness or to increase its destructive force, as to lend a certain keenness to the wit, thereby making it more than ever a *tour de force*. He does not use his irony to give vigorous expression to his criticisms of his neighbours; he directs it at opinion rather than behaviour, and the strongest sentiment that accompanies it is the contempt that belongs to intellectual aloofness. There is but little genuine indignation apparent in Arbuthnot's writing; but where it is to be found, irony is absent; for the irony which accompanies strong emotion would be too bitter for that sensitive and kindly nature. Only in *The Memoirs of Scriblerus* is there anything approaching a savage irony, and in this Swift had a considerable share. Perhaps the most successful of Arbuthnot's ironical works is the essay on *The Art of Political Lying*.

...Here the author makes a digression in praise of the Whig party, for the right understanding and use of proof-lies. A proof-lie is like a proof-charge for a piece of ordnance, to try a standard credulity. Of such a nature he takes transubstantiation to be, in the Church of Rome, a proof-

55

article, which, if anyone swallows, they are sure he will digest anything else: therefore the Whig party do wisely to try the credulity of the people by swingers, that they may be able to judge to what height they may charge them afterwards. Towards the end of this chapter he warns the heads of parties against believing their own lies, which has proved of pernicious consequence of late, both a wise party and a wise nation having regulated their affairs upon lies of their own invention. The causes of this he supposes to be too great a zeal and intenseness in the practice of this art, and a vehement heat in mutual conversation, whereby they persuade one another that what they wish, and report to be true, is really so: that all parties have been subject to this misfortune. The Jacobites have been constantly infested with it; but the Whigs of late seemed even to exceed them in this ill habit and weakness. To this chapter the author subjoins a calendar of lies, proper for the several months of the year.

In 1735 Pulteney wrote to Swift, 'Poor Arbuthnot, who grieved to see the wickedness of mankind, and was particularly ashamed of his own countrymen, is dead— quite weary of the world and tired of such bad company.' Swift had to face another ten years of life in Dublin, his madness increasing, and Pope also survived another nine years, but Matthew Prior and Gay were both dead; and so, in 1735, the brilliant circle, wherein irony had so greatly flourished and obtained a unique prominence, was finally broken up. Already the ascendancy of Addison and Steele (Addison had died in 1719) had shown that a new element was to arise in English literature, a reflective element of a kinder and more tolerant nature. For society was at length settling down; it began to realise that Time had worked his cure, and

56

that the forms of social hostilities were outliving the dissensions from which they had sprung.

That Arbuthnot, in most cases, reserved his irony for the regions of wit is a very significant thing; he kept it out of sterner criticism, and was thus prophetic of the age about to dawn. Addison and Steele had, in their different ways, worked for the same end. They revived in people a sense of kindliness and tolerance that the long succession of past strife had dried up; they had a profoundly humanising influence, not on literature alone, but on their age in general. *The Spectator* hastened the end of the first and heartless period of the Age of Wit. Moreover, the peace of Walpole's administration gave society an opportunity to settle down; longstanding suspicions diminished, and the sentimentalism, kindled by *The Spectator*, gained ground, reaching its consummation in Richardson, and, in a different way, in Sterne. This element usurped the place that irony had formerly held in the more serious departments of social criticism. The former harshness seemed unnecessary now, and in these quieter times a sober criticism replaced the passionate denunciation of Swift. There is a sentence of Sterne's in *The Sentimental Journey* that, as it seems to us, epitomises the new spirit: 'I walked gravely to the window in my dusty black coat, and looking through the glass saw all the world in yellow, blue, and green, running at the ring of pleasure.' The extraordinary success of *Pamela* showed how vigorously people had reacted from the old order; henceforth reform must be gained not by chastisement but from an appeal to the heart. The Sentimentalists kept a charitable watch over society, and directed their appeals as occasion seemed to demand.

In this way it would appear that the ground was cut from beneath the feet of irony. The Sentimentalists had little to say for it, but to their disinclination was added an inability to use it, for they had not a sufficient sense of the ridiculous. This, indeed, the wits, who remained monopolists in irony, possessed, so far as their limited idea of humour would allow. Goldsmith, discussing humour, commits himself to the most surprising admissions.

'The critic,' he said, 'by demanding an impossibility of the comic poet, has, in effect, banished true comedy from the stage. This he has done by banning low subjects, and by prescribing the comic or satirical muse from every walk but higher life, which, though abounding in fools as well as the humbler station, is by no means so fruitful in absurdity. Absurdity is the comic poet's game and good breeding is the nice concealment of absurdity. The truth is, the critic usually mistakes humour for wit, which is a very different excellence; wit raises human nature above its level; humour acts a contrary part and equally depresses it. To expect exalted humour is a contradiction in terms. . .the poet must place the object he would have for subject of his humour in a state of inferiority; in other words the subject of humour must be low.'

It will be sad for irony if it falls into the hands of people holding these views. Humour is built upon sympathy, and irony lavished upon trivialities without the imaginative sympathy of humour is the dreariest of all the productions of intolerance. Higher life in Goldsmith's time was, of course, abundantly fruitful in absurdity. Modern sociability was then a new thing, and it was very self-satisfied and very self-conscious. Being thus restricted in freedom, society was perfectly incapable of perceiving a joke in itself; for it could not escape from itself. Consequently, its sense of the ridiculous was confined to things which it conceived to be inferior to itself; and this was extremely appropriate, for it liked feeling superior. Many evils will befall irony in such a society; the laugh of superiority is the oldest of all laughs, but it has little to do with the comic, and it is but an infinitesimal part of humour, if it is any part of it at all. Fortunately, before the mild Goldsmith had made his atrocious statement about humour, Fielding had already arisen to save irony in its grave danger.

Fielding has a place in the history of English irony second only to Swift; early as he stands among our novelists, his work, nevertheless, possesses a vivacity that makes it very readable still, and there is something about his characters singularly true to human nature in spite of their many absurdities and overdrawn propensities. We will, however, leave him, together with other ironical novelists, for consideration in a later chapter; for the present we must continue to trace the progress of prophetic irony in the hands of writers, who did not choose to avail themselves of the special facilities that the novel offers for the exposure of folly and of vice.

CHAPTER V

THE FURTHER PROGRESS
OF PROPHETIC IRONY

We left irony in danger owing to two extreme tendencies in literature. The sentimental Humorist, who sought to frustrate whatever he disliked by an appeal to the emotions, had neither the inclination nor the right kind of ability for the use of irony. The Wit, on the other hand, had both the inclination and the ability, but he lacked the essential kindness of heart and sympathy, without which it is a dangerous thing to indulge in irony. A sense of humour might have saved the situation, but the age of wit was far from being an age of humour. What irony needed was some one with the Wit's sense of the ridiculous and the Sentimentalist's warmth of heart: such a man would be a true Humorist. Perhaps he would use irony but little, but he would use it well; and that is all that is necessary.

In Dr Johnson it seems that the wit and the sentimentalist have come together at last. If we do not think of him as a great humorist it is because he is also so majestic. There can be no doubt about his wit. In speech it was as brutal as it was triumphant; it was a weapon with which he knocked objectors down, impatient of any argument, though it must be remembered that conversation was a game in which one talked for victory. Dr Johnson's writings bear no trace of such brutality; his wit does not disappear, but the kindliness and the great-heartedness of the moralist outshine it.

In early life **Dr Johnson** wrote two ironical works on comical subjects, called *Marmor Norfolciense* and *A Complete Vindication of the Licensors of the Stage*. They were not at all successful, for Johnson had not the gift of sustained irony: very few people have. He soon, however, learnt the folly of his ways. Continued irony is only very rarely possible; there are occasions, when with a really adequate subject, it can be effective, but great skill is necessary, and a lightness and brilliance of style that is not Johnson's. It may be witty and amusing, but hardly decorous and dignified, and Johnson's writings and the type of literature which he epitomises owe their charm to their decorum and dignity. And so the author of *Marmor Norfolciense* came to reserve his irony for what appeared to him to be extreme cases of folly—vice was too serious a matter—and he produces it so cleverly at times that for a moment it is hardly discernible amidst the humour that surrounds it. The following quotation is Dr Johnson's animadversion upon a notion in a book on *The Origin of Evil* by Soame Jenyns. That hasty philosopher had the misfortune to observe that, as we use animals for our diversion, so may superior beings 'deceive, torment or destroy us for the ends only of their own pleasure.' The Doctor's retort is well known, and it is significant that it has often been given as an example of his humour; it is equally adequate as an example of his irony.

I cannot resist the temptation of contemplating this analogy, which I think he might have carried a little further, very much to the advantage of his argument. He might have shown that these 'hunters, whose game is man,' may have sports analogous to our own. As we drown whelps or kittens, they amuse themselves with sinking a ship, and stand round the fields of Blenheim, or the walls of Prague as we encircle a cock-pit. As we shoot a bird flying, they take a man in the midst of his business or pleasure, and knock him down with an apoplexy. Some of them, perhaps, are 'virtuosi,' and delight in the operations of an asthma, as a human philosopher in the effects of an air-pump. Many a merry bout have these frolick beings at the vicissitudes of an ague, and good sport it is to see a man tumble with an epilepsy, and revive and tumble again, and all this he knows not why. . . . The paroxysms of the gout and stone must undoubtedly make high mirth, especially if the play be a little diversified with the blunders and puzzles of the blind and deaf. . . . One sport the merry malice of these beings has found means of enjoying, to which we have nothing equal or similar. They now and then catch a mortal, proud of his parts, and flattered either by the submission of those who court his kindness, or the notice of those who suffer him to court theirs. A head thus prepared for the reception of false opinions and the projection of vain designs, they easily fill with idle notions till, in time, they make their plaything an author; their first diversion commonly begins with an ode or an epistle, then rises perhaps to a political irony, and is at last brought to its height by a treatise of philosophy. Then begins the poor animal to entangle himself in sophisms and to flounder in absurdity.

No one could call this friendly criticism, and yet to a sojourner in the age of wit, Dr Johnson's irony must have seemed refreshingly playful and lacking in spite. There is plenty of humour in it, or rather, with it, for irony is not, and can never be made, a form of humour. It is criticism, full of understanding, but without sympathy; and when an author becomes ironical in the midst of humour, he is in fact exchanging humour for wit. These comparisons may be dangerous and often misleading, for it is rash to generalise where motive, subject and circumstance are all-important, but there remains some distinctive quality about irony which compels us to acknowledge it a guest and not a native in the land of humour. Humour is frank and spontaneous; irony has always about it a suggestion of cunning, of malice aforethought. No one can be ironised without feeling that advantage has been taken of him, whether in play or earnest. Fortunately for irony there are occasions when a little cunning, used judiciously, is an admirable thing and can succeed where no amount of laughter, direct mockery, argument, or denunciation would be likely to do so. And even humour, kindly though it be, will not hesitate to encourage irony now and again, in cases where a little medicine seems necessary.

Although Dr Johnson used his irony 'to expose the fool' rather than 'to lash the knave,' as an ironist he must be numbered amongst the prophets. His claim to be so considered may seem at first a little doubtful. But it must be remembered that in his time rationalism had carried thought into many fantastic and absurd regions. This tendency of empiricism is, indeed, one of the ironies of life: Warburton's application of the original contract theory to nearly every department of life, Dr Clarke's innumerable dogmas concerning the attributes of God, and, on a lower grade, the ridiculous analogy of Soame Jenyns already mentioned, these and many other ideas current at that time point to an age of mental acrobatics performed upon no sure foundation. It was against this looseness of thought that Johnson set his heart. His professed dislike of metaphysic was his manner of expressing his devotion to simple and clear thinking; his admiration for common sense was his way of saying that simple faith is very preferable to scepticism born of intellectual conceit rather than of genuine doubt. His creed was that of simplicity and sincerity of mind, and a firm belief that it is best for people not to meddle with things they do not understand; and it was on behalf of this creed that he used his irony. Dr Johnson tried to effect with dignity and patience what Swift, more like a prophet perhaps, did passionately and heedlessly. But Swift laboured under greater provocation. The age of Johnson was golden compared with that of Swift.

When Dr Johnson died, the ominous symptoms of the social evils resulting from the Industrial Revolution were already very apparent. Then suddenly to this gathering unrest was added the terrific impetus of the French Revolution. Burke, the vile Whig and generous philosopher, whose relations with Dr Johnson are so attractive and human an episode in literary history, succumbed to the general panic, and gave voice to his essential conservatism in the greatest condemnation of revolutionary methods ever written. The *Reflections on the Revolution in France* abound in irony of a very high order, despite the violence of Burke's passionate alarm

64

which too often invades the book. Yet on the whole it may be said of him, and not of Swift or even of Milton, that his wrath, although it lost him personal respect and not infrequently hurried him into gross metaphor, nevertheless gave such fire to his expression that the gain was greater than the loss. 'It scathed like lightning,' wrote Mr Payne, 'the men, the systems, and the sentiments which were the objects of his moral indignation, and marked indelibly those who incurred his personal resentment.' Needless to say, it is best when it scathes systems and sentiments, and worst when it attacks individuals.

Burke is very like Milton: only too often he begins a passage in a strain of suppressed anger condensed into irony, but soon passion breaks through and the irony is abandoned for unmistakable abuse.

Such schemes [i.e. the military dispositions of the French revolutionary Assembly] are not like propositions coming from a man of fifty years wear and tear amongst mankind. They seem rather such as ought to be expected from those grand compounders in politics, who shorten the road to their degrees in the state; and have a certain inward assurance and illumination upon all subjects; upon the credit of which one of their doctors has thought fit, with great applause and greater success, to caution the assembly not to attend to old men, or to any persons who valued themselves upon their experience. I suppose all ministers of state must qualify and take this test; wholly abjuring the errors and heresies of experience and observation. Every man has his relish. But I think, if I could not attain to the wisdom, I would at least preserve something of the stiff and peremptory dignity of old age. These gentlemen deal in regeneration;

but at any price I should hardly yield my rigid fibres to be regenerated by them; nor begin, in my grand climacteric, to squall in their new accents, or to stammer in my second cradle the elemental sounds of their barbarous metaphysics. *Si isti mihi largiantur ut repuerescam, et in eorum cunis vagiam, valde recusem.*

Just as Burke cannot long maintain an euphemistic disguise, but casts it off and roundly declares his disgust, so his irony, when it takes the form of assumed deprecation, fades away as his admiration for the subject gathers force. His famous defence of prejudice is a good example.

You see, Sir, in this enlightened age I am bold enough to confess that we [i.e. the English contrasted with the French] are generally men of untaught feelings; that instead of casting away all our old prejudices, we cherish them to a very considerable degree, and to take more shame to ourselves, we cherish them because they are prejudices; and the longer they have lasted, and the more generally they have prevailed, the more we cherish them. We are afraid to put men to live and trade each on his own private stock of reason; because we suspect that this stock in each man is small, and that the individuals would do better to avail themselves of the general bank and capital of nations and of ages. Many of our men of speculation, instead of exploding general prejudices, employ their sagacity to discover the latent wisdom which prevails in them. If they find what they seek (and they seldom fail), they think it more wise to continue the prejudice, with the reason involved, than to cast away the coat of prejudice, and to leave nothing but the naked reason; because prejudice with its reason has a motive to give to that reason, and an affection which will give it permanence.

66

The fact is that Burke is too impulsive for subdued, and too impatient for sustained, irony. His irony is seldom cumulative, yet it is never purely incidental; it is never a passing criticism, it is always combative and pointed. Burke's irony could never be called 'little' irony; it is excess of emotion, and not indifference or amiability, that cuts it short. His readers will have noticed that his irony occurs at the moment when, in the course of the argument, he is led to touch upon something which calls forth a sudden access of feeling. On such occasions, Burke seems, as if by nature, to seek for a moment ironical speech. But whereas Swift, with swelling indignation, would gather the forces of his imagination and carry his irony to a ruthless conclusion, Burke quickly tires of a method so indirect; his fancy envisages the object of his distaste, and irony abandoned, he must smother and submerge the enormity beneath a fury of description, that is sometimes almost frenzied and, only too often, unjust. In all this he resembles Milton, and the similarity between the two is not without significance in the history of irony, seeing that they both lived in an age of revolution and extreme social unrest. With both of them, their amazing nobility of language is unable to atone at times for their savagery, but just as Milton sinks lower than Burke in fierce vindictiveness, so also he rises higher in noble restraint; consequently there are pieces of irony in the *Areopagitica* which the Irishman could never hope to emulate. There is, however, one kind of restraint which Burke uses with great effect at times. While it is not irony, it is a kindred phenomenon; it is, at any rate, more than a mere trick of *meiosis*. Sometimes, after much elaboration and accumulation of the facts that make up his premiss, he states his inference in terms that are, by contrast, unemphatic. We cannot resist giving an example of this which reveals Burke as an extraordinary writer of English, although not, in this instance, an ironist.

Indeed, when I consider the face of the Kingdom of France, the multitude and opulence of her cities; the useful magnificence of her spacious high roads and bridges; the opportunity of her artificial canals and navigations opening the conveniences of maritime communication through a solid continent of so immense an extent; when I turn my eyes to the stupendous works of her ports and harbours, and to her whole naval apparatus, whether for war or trade; when I bring before my view the number of her fortifications constructed with so bold and masterly a skill, and made and maintained at so prodigious a charge, presenting an armed front and impenetrable barrier to her enemies upon every side; when I recollect how very small a part of that extensive region is without cultivation, and to what complete perfection the culture of many of the best productions of the earth have been brought in France; when I reflect on the excellence of her manufactures and fabrics, second to none but ours, and in some particulars not second; when I contemplate the grand foundations of charity, public and private; when I survey the state of all the arts that beautify and polish life; when I reckon the men she has bred for extending her fame in war, her able statesmen, the multitude of her profound lawyers and theologians, her philosophers, her critics, her historians and antiquaries, her poets, her orators, sacred and profane, I behold in all this something which awes and commands the imagination, which checks

68

the mind on the brink of precipitate and indiscriminate censure, and which demands that we should seriously examine what and how great are the latent vices that could authorise us at once to level so spacious a fabric to the ground. I do not recognise, in this view of things, the despotism of Turkey. Nor do I discern the character of a government, that has been, on the whole, so oppressive, or so corrupt, or so negligent, as to be utterly unfit *for all reformation.* I must think such a government well deserved to have its excellencies heightened; its faults corrected; and its capacities improved into a British constitution.

There is no irony here, but the suppression at the end, as for instance in the sentence: *I do not recognise, in this view of things, the despotism of Turkey,* coming after so much elaboration, has about it an emotional intenseness, with which we become very familiar in ironical speech, and there is an implied rebuke for those who venture to disagree with the writer, which is something very like irony. It is a favourite trick of Burke.

But the cases are many where what is loosely called 'ironic feeling' is suggested without the definite employment of irony. With some writers, as with Edward Gibbon, this is constantly occuring; his temperament seems steeped in all those mental characteristics which most easily lead to the employment of irony, until at length his readers can never be certain that their grandiloquent author has not his tongue in his cheek. Burke, at any rate, does not resemble Gibbon in this respect; his irony is always the irony of rhetoric; but his passion is genuine and not rhetorically feigned. *Meiosis* is the keynote of his irony; a *meiosis* with difficulty achieved, and often unsuccessful. He knows that to say a little is often the most effective thing; but that little, embittered with irony and bursting with suffocating wrath, inadequately conceals the verbal torrents that are piling up behind it, and not infrequently break through in full flood.

The wide and far-reaching social unrest that maintained its intensity until the triumph of utilitarianism, and the reaction from the Chartist movement, did not result in that output of ironical writing that one might have expected; in part, perhaps, because the nature and causes of the trouble were too indefinite or too imperfectly understood for the incisive treatment of irony; and also because the Romanticism of the age did not encourage irony. There is a spirit of rebellion about Romanticism which calls often for impassioned and vehement speech. The largeness of the subject has compelled us to confine ourselves in this essay to works of prose, otherwise there would be much in the works of the English revolutionary poets that would demand consideration. The irony of Shelley and Byron is at times magnificent. But there is another aspect of Romanticism which seems inconducive of ironical speech, and akin to much that is essential in the outlook of the humorist. Romanticism is concerned far more with appreciation than with criticism. Thus Wordsworth would deprecate, but not convict; he would laugh, but not ridicule; and if he condemned, he would not pursue.

The indignation that arose against the social oppression of those days was very passionate, but also, in the nature of things, sentimental rather than intellectual. Humanitarianism has little use for irony, and it leaves no opportunity for controversy. People like Tom Payne and Cobbett said many hard things, but they said them simply and directly; and, in another sphere, *The Song of the Shirt* did more than any amount of formal denunciation could have accomplished.

Irony likes a definite issue, but since the beginning of the nineteenth century, and the dawn of what may be called modern conditions, it seems that definite issues must grow increasingly few. A great complication surrounds all questions; the problems of life remain the same, but their application to detail becomes obscured in the growing complexity. The issues are there, just as the many obstinate heresies, against which irony might with profit be launched, are also present; but they lie concealed beneath a mass of superficial vaguenesses, and it is hard to find them, harder still to expose them with that vivid certainty that the ironist must possess. The man who can do both these things is indeed a prophet.

Samuel Butler had in abundance the insight that perceives the fundamental questions lying beneath the superficial morass; and he was, moreover, a past master in the use of irony. From the standpoint of the technique of the ironist, a comparison of *Erewhon* and *Gulliver's Travels* would be very much to the purpose; it must, however, be sufficient here to say that Butler has not quite the skill of Swift in mingling his narrative with his ironical exposition, which fall into alternating sections, and are both quite admirable in their way. Butler is hampered by the fact that he deals with questions of a far more philosophic nature than those which agitated the mind of Swift. Nevertheless, the book contains a quantity of topical irony that is unsurpassed in its own way, and exceedingly good-humoured and witty. It is, however, when he is treating such simple failings as beset men of all ages that he really excels himself:

I write with great diffidence, but it seems to me that there is no unfairness in punishing people for their misfortunes, or rewarding them for sheer good luck: it is the normal condition of human life that this should be done, and no rightminded person will complain of being subjected to the common treatment. There is no alternative open to us. It is idle to say that men are not responsible for their misfortunes. What is responsibility? Surely to be responsible means to be liable to have to give an answer should it be demanded, and all things which live are responsible for their lives and actions should society see fit to question them through the mouth of its authorised agents.

If Butler is not the greatest of our political ironists, he may well be considered by his admirers to be the most attractive. And he is, perhaps, the most recent of them. Since his day irony has not vanished from our literature, but it has become assimilated and informal. In many ways Butler seems to belong to an earlier age.

Surveying once more the course of prophetic irony in England, we see that, beginning with Milton, there follows a remarkable concurrence of great ironists, among whom Swift and Defoe stand pre-eminent. Thereafter the ironic flame dies down with the quietening of the times, but conspicuous moralists, amongst whom are Johnson, Fielding and Burke, occasionally avail themselves of the ironic artillery. Meanwhile Fielding, having discovered a new method, subjects it to a more frequent use. Such bombardments, when direct methods fail, or provocation demands something more than purely reasonable dissuasion, seem to us to be the most natural and proper sphere to which those who would use irony in formal denunciation should confine themselves. Such irony may rightly be called prophetic, for the prophet is one who comes to turn the hearts of a stiff-necked generation. But just as there are major and minor prophets, just as the main issues of social life are more or less imperative, and more or less clear, so does denunciation fade into criticism, and even criticism subside at times into good-humoured banter. In the same way prophetic irony with its occasional justification, and the 'little' irony which is sufficiently mingled with humour, and the kindliness that humour implies, to be appropriate whenever man has the ability to use it, are simply the two extremes of what might be called the ironic gradation. Somewhere in the midst of this gradation stands Samuel Butler. He was a prophet in an age when prophecy was not unneeded: but the complication of modern life multiplied for him the issues which many less penetrating minds were unable even to perceive. He therefore adopted no conspicuous battle-cries, nor are we to suppose that he had any such desire, for in an urbane age Butler could compete with most in respect of urbanity. We find him the politest of prophets, a seer who never loses his temper: he is not indignant, and the passion that we associate with the prophet is lacking in him; he prosecutes but does not scourge, and in this respect he joins hands with Daniel Defoe and parts company with Jonathan Swift and Edmund Burke. Yet prophesy he does, and his smaller ironies pass easily into indictments of his age that are stern, however dispassionate.

Butler was able to look down upon his own generation with something of the gaze that Gibbon fixed upon a world a thousand years before his time. That this is a very rare achievement accounts for the comparative scarcity of prophetic irony in any literature; but it does not explain what appears to be the spontaneous accession of ironic activity that overwhelmed English literature in the Restoration period and culminated in Swift and his contemporaries. It may well be that, amidst the moral degeneration and scepticism of that time, nothing could succeed in awakening people to the desirability of better standards so well as a vigorous use of irony. Although, as we think, the extent of this abandonment of principles before the shrines of pleasure and ambition has been exaggerated, a certain section of society being regarded unfairly as representative of the whole, there can be no doubt that anything approaching an age of irony denotes unhealthiness of some kind in society. Yet any society, during a period of unhealthiness, can still exhibit in its actions much that is characteristic of peculiarities in themselves healthy enough, quite apart

74

from whether these actions are remedial or no. It is unnecessary therefore, and, as we think, untrue to attribute the irony of these men purely to the circumstances of their age. In other countries, as, for instance, in France at a period no less unsatisfactory in her social history, comedy rather than satire has been made the vehicle of prophetic criticism. Now comedy is very conducive to the milder uses of irony, as we to-day know well; but in the early eighteenth century, when the authority of classical models was very great, it was Cicero and Demosthenes rather than any comedian who seemed a pattern for ironists, for the original connection of irony with rhetoric and controversy was still influential. It was only in downright, combatant irony that people recognised a definite literary form, and this irony is far more easily combined with satire than with comedy. It is a peculiarity of the English, and of English literature, that, in the eighteenth century at any rate, we preferred satire to comedy. With this preference, as we pointed out in an earlier chapter, the irony that is distinctively an English product is closely concerned. Satire is a somewhat brutal form of literature, and, as such, it runs easily into formal, unrelenting irony. But our great ironists, while not afraid to use their heavy guns realised that they had found an instrument of criticism that excelled satire itself in range and adaptability. Irony may well serve as satire's heavy artillery: she serves no less well as the humour of satire. The frequent savagery of Swift has obscured for many people the magnificent use that he makes of irony in

75

this latter sense. Defoe can never equal Swift in either of these two uses of irony, or, indeed, in any other use, but by his unfailing good temper he did as much as anyone to show that irony, the natural intensifier of satire, can also be used to soften this rather cumbrous and morose weapon of literature. This, in an age of satire, was valuable service.

The influence of irony upon English literature at its most ironical period is thus curiously complex. Violent irony served only to make the confusion of satire worse confounded; gentle and amusing irony was hardly abundant enough to help people to escape for a moment out of the rather heartless atmosphere of the age of wit and to learn better manners, though it strove valiantly to accomplish this; while, from time to time, stern and well-directed irony assisted the general raising of standards in a somewhat decadent age. From the English standpoint, at any rate from the standpoint of two hundred years ago, comedy is rather elaborate and verbose. Our proverbial reticence may be an illusion, but in criticism we have always preferred to be direct and to the point, and have mistrusted indirect methods however ingenious and witty, as though they must always be the result of cowardice, and never of a sense of delicacy struggling with a determination not to let the obnoxious thing go unrebuked. But there comes a point beyond which direct criticism cannot be pushed without endangering the precarious concord of society. Satire is at best a poor disguise, and we found in irony a means of criticism which avoided too brutal a directness, and which could be used either with impressive dignity or with something very near to humour, as occasion might demand.

But the suitability of irony from the point of view of its users was not alone responsible for its frequency. It was the great popularity of the method which made the pen of Swift a weapon to be feared. Aristocratic government was established in England at a time when that aristocracy was supremely disunited. The society which desired to consider itself polite society was divided on every question; on religion, politics, and philosophy in their most fundamental aspect, no less than on the different topical issues in which circumstances presented these problems at the moment. Despite the cry for religious toleration, the disjointed aristocracy was scarcely more willing to tolerate the opinions of its conflicting members than it was the putting of these opinions into practice. Increasing scepticism, while it did not heal the religious breach, at any rate made the controversies arising therefrom less acutely polemical, but politics did not experience to the full this deadening influence. A pose of scepticism was never unfashionable in the first half of the eighteenth century, but beneath it a strong current of political feeling animated all classes, and amongst the aristocracy this feeling was intensely personal. Hence the ironist need not fear to make political enemies, for he would make as many friends. If one portion of society saw with indignation the humiliation of their principles and their public men at the hand of the ironist, their opponents applauded the spectacle and found it an occasion for protracted mirth; and on either side there were great men in plenty, able and willing to extend the strong and protecting arm of patronage.

This state of affairs, while it created a demand that led the better writers to examine and improve the technique of irony, was not without its disadvantages, for it called into being a breed of journalists, who, being admittedly time-servers, offered the assistance of their pens to the highest bidders, and made it their business to pour forth, to order, their torrents of political obloquy. Such men acquired a partisan popularity only in proportion to the combative efficiency of their productions; justice of opinion and literary merit, if they had any, counted for little. But more independent and sincere writers obtained genuine admiration for a successful display of irony. Defoe's exposure at the pillory was for him a veritable triumph. The friendly mob that transformed his punishment had perhaps greater hatred of ecclesiastical arrogance than appreciation of ironic subtleties; but we must not suppose that the popularity of irony sprang only from the gratification of factions. In irony that is worthy of the name there are two essential qualities that could not fail to make an especial appeal to the age of wit. There is, in the first place, the dexterity and cleverness of presentment which that age so greatly admired; and there is an appeal to common sense and common fairness which, in the midst of a diversity of antagonisms, could not fail to delight and refresh the majority of men, however much the people who felt themselves injured by it experienced an increase of dudgeon and resentment against their accusers. It is the minor prophets of this world who make the most successful ironists, and minor prophets are not without honour, even in their own countries. Especially will this be the case when they live amongst a people whose power of coherent speech declines as its emotion increases. The fervent dumb will welcome the prophetic safety-valve.

The pessimist does not hesitate to declare that the cosmopolitanism of modern times has combined with the degeneration of the national stock to make us a more garrulous and less reflective people. Those who agree may find in this a further reason for the disappearance of prophetic irony to-day. Prophets are bores, and we are impatient of them unless they can conceal their prophecy in a novel. No generation, however, can pass judgment on itself: we must be content to observe that the old prophetic irony is dead and gone. Society is as disordered as it ever was, but class distinctions have replaced the divisions of the aristocracy; and it is a fortunate thing that ironical declamations do not adorn these graceless hostilities.

The irony that belongs to modern literature is in no sense distinctively English, although the influence of Gibbon is still apparent. Irony divorced from prophecy gained freedom, if it lost in bulk and importance. Being used less often as an instrument of formal criticism, it has grown more incidental and occasional. It has at the same time become far more plastic and expressive of personal taste, and being connected more frequently with the minor criticisms of life that spring from individual caprice, it has disclosed amiable and humorous potentialities that more than atone for its dethronement from a position, which, while imposing, was perhaps always inclined to be a little forced and unnatural, and sprang from the unusual circumstances of a somewhat tiresome age. But we must leave the progress of 'little' irony to the next chapter

CHAPTER VI
IRONY IN NARRATIVE

I

THE NOVELIST

The particular advantages that the novel affords the ironist were recognised by Swift in *Gulliver's Travels*, and, to a smaller extent, by Arbuthnot in *The History of John Bull*; but neither of these works, nor yet *Erewhon* itself, can be called a novel. *Jonathan Wild*, on the other hand, although no less palpably a piece of satire, somehow deserves the name. It is difficult to discover quite what it is that makes Fielding's book so different in character, for if ever there was a story told for a purpose it is this one; and, with the exception of Mr and Mrs Heartfree, the people who attend upon Jonathan's remarkable career are bad enough to turn Arbuthnot's wild personalities into saints, while their behaviour is as fantastically impossible. The fact remains that these surprising creatures are not personifications, they are people; no matter how incredible their conduct, the author has infused into them the breath of life. Jonathan Wild is perhaps Fielding's masterpiece as an engine of irony; he is, at any rate, a very interesting—we had almost said attractive—person, and if he had not been so sensible about it, it would be even more distressing than it is to see him hanged.

Once an author can make his characters live, it is not difficult to understand how great an opportunity for ironical utterance lies open to him. We have seen to what straits the essayist is put; how he must simulate amiability, and dissimulate his natural indignation however passionate, or his contempt however profound; and even then the fate may befall him, which befell Burke in his youth, when he wrote an ironical essay with such singular cunning and so laudable a restraint, that no one knew it to be ironical at all, and many were surprised at the soundness of the author's opinions. A novelist who can create living people is spared this pain and trouble; his characters, so they be worthy of the name, are between him and his readers, and their vitality will conceal his ultimate control;—ultimate, indeed, because he cannot have it all his own way; if he makes his characters alive, he must let them live. And yet there can surely be little excuse for an author who allows the children of his pen to lord it over him; he can threaten them with long obscurity, with suspended animation, to say nothing of total extinction; but in these soft times an author is so kind-hearted; and his books tell of his sad oppression, his dislocated control. He cannot save himself, it seems; or is he prepared to put up with the oppression and to proclaim his domestic anarchy, so long as his Bolshevik offspring shall dance before the public eye?

The ironist, however, is usually a disciplinarian (the fruit of that cynicism which springs from failure is not true irony); he is a Providence in his own sphere, remembering that he has made nothing that he cannot destroy. The essayist, who is also an ironist, will take care to wrap his irony in a cloak of genuine amiability;

he may lash the particular, but he loves the whole. He must preserve that saving sense of proportion that humour alone can give; he must stand outside himself; he must view with the unswerving scrutiny of the Comic Spirit the man who has dared to invoke the aid of irony against another, and he will find the moments are not frequent when the humorist can make use of irony and conscientiously preserve his self-esteem entirely unruffled. In fiction, in an author's treatment of his characters, the case is less extreme; we can pardon more; indeed, we relish a certain amount; we are very indulgent, just as we are of Nemesis and the Irony of Fate, when it does not touch us too closely ourselves. Indeed, it is the business of an author to be a diminutive Providence in his own sphere, and we allow him an equal proportion of divine privilege. This is the secret of Miss Austen's charm; she is a Providence indeed; and it is irresistibly pleasant to observe a young lady (for Miss Austen is always young) delivering her providential reproofs. We do not refer to her management of the plot, but to the running commentary with which she caresses, encourages, or upbraids her characters, as they walk her lively stage. Her irony is quick as lightning; it flashes and is gone; it is triumphant; it is gloriously allusive, and we feel the sting of it ourselves; but we can only laugh, for it is 'little' irony, and the wide embrace of humour is around it. Miss Austen's art is consummate, and few could achieve what she has achieved; she has, nevertheless, displayed the essential suitability of the novel for that light and amiable use of

83   6-2

irony, which it is so difficult to imitate in the more direct forms of literary expression. Irony is least brutal, in proportion as it is least direct; it thrives in a world of imagery and fancy; and a novel is, in a sense, nothing but fancy, and the characters are images of the author's mind.

Very different is Fielding. He does not use his irony to buffet his characters and, through them, to cast an incidental criticism upon his contemporaries; he makes his characters themselves the engines of a very penetrating irony. The people in Fielding's books, with the exception of a few like Parson Adams, are caricatures; their very names betray them, and yet at the same time they have individuality and are full of life; herein lies his especial genius. His irony is general and not personal, but it gains in intensity by being the product of these caricatures, who are also people. It is a very subtle method.

Fielding's history is significant in two ways: in the first place he started by writing, or trying to write, comedy, and gave it up; in the second place, his first attempt at irony was aimed at an individual, namely Richardson, and this too proved unsuitable; and so *The Adventures of Joseph Andrews* are allowed to become centred around the attractive character of Parson Adams. Fielding discovered that it was no good to attack *Pamela* in which there is so much that is admirable, for in that case though the good is dragged into the mire along with the bad, it will not suffer so much as the injudicious irony that attacks it. Fielding did not object to what was best in Richardson; no one can, for it is pure idealism; but he did very strongly decry the common tendency to regard virtue and respectability as the same thing, a tendency which Richardson had not discouraged. *Jonathan Wild* is launched directly against this heresy; a 'prig' and a thief are assumed to be identical, and only Mr Heartfree, the virtuous man, is admirable, 'for if not, let some other kind of man be admirable; as Jonathan Wild,' in whom every grace of manner and a gentleman's 'honour' were combined; but unfortunately he was entirely dishonest. It is a very brisk *reductio ad absurdum*. The only other character in fiction comparable to Jonathan Wild as an instrument of irony is Sir Willoughby Patterne, but he owes it partly to his attendant imps; Jonathan Wild needs no such support.

If on the side of Fielding and of irony we have Meredith and Jane Austen, it cannot escape notice that many novelists, and those the greatest, have followed Richardson; they need the positive sense of his idealism. The idealist, indeed, is prone to be a sentimentalist; the great artist is content to paint things as they are, and they will read their own lesson; he has no need of indirect methods. The burlesque that irony provides is, in a sense, an admission that direct vision is failing, that men have eyes and see not. Dickens is the greatest of Richardson's successors, and, in our own day, there is Mr Galsworthy. Their wide experience does not ignore the spice of life, but they lack the sense of perversity that animates the ironist; just as Thackeray and all great humorists stop short of the gentle malignity that the ironist is not ashamed now and again to enjoy.

We spoke, in the previous chapter, of the blow that prophetic irony has suffered in the disappearance of definite issues and the growing complexity of life; but will this account for the comparative scarcity of 'little' irony in the novels of to-day? On the contrary, it should encourage it, for complication results in an excess of absurdity. In these regions, it is true, irony must compete with the Comic Spirit, but with this spirit 'little irony,' at any rate, has been long in alliance, being, as it were, her heavy artillery. We offer the following solution of the problem with diffidence. Science has blunted our sense of the ridiculous, or rather, we have allowed science, which is not to blame, to have this effect upon us. We cannot know too much of the causes of things, but we allow our fast increasing knowledge of causes to trespass on our sense of value. A thing is ridiculous not simply because it cannot be justified by reason, but because it springs from a disproportionate sense of value; moreover, it remains the same, either good or bad, sensible or absurd, whatever causes may have been responsible for its state. For this reason, if a person be ridiculous, he deserves our laughter, whether or no 'a sex complex' or an irritable parent have contributed to his derangement. This is not unkind, for laughter need not be unkind, and irony too should be provocative rather than malicious. Slight provocation at times is a very good thing; for provoked absurdity has a way of exploding.

These things the modern novelist will not see: too much knowledge has made him mad. Personified complexes dominate his soul and goad him to a fearful fatality. He dare not laugh at things which are so solemn, for it would be high treason against the Immortal Cause. He has not the heart to direct his irony against diseases of the mind and ailments of the soul. What is laughable, he says, were it not so detestable, is this primitive belief in tonics, in being braced, when what we really need are the soothing explanations of the psycho-analyst. Perhaps we do, but not at the expense of that freedom of the mind which is born of mirth. Laughter may be deeply related to the 'superiority complex,' but it is the salt of the earth.

II

BIOGRAPHY

We must leave the novelist to consider his two relatives in irony, the historian and the biographer. This relationship is short-lived; it consists in the fact that all three of them are 'telling a story,' in the one case fictitious, in the others, it may be hoped, true; and their irony belongs to a class which has been called, at the head of this chapter, 'Irony in Narrative,' as opposed to the irony of essayists and apologists, which we have already discussed. But apart from this common tie, a divergence begins to appear, in the first place between the novelist on the one hand and the historian and the biographer on the other, and later between the historian and the biographer themselves. All three of them are concerned with the portrayal of human nature, but whereas two of them draw from actual life, the novelist makes an imaginary picture, relying for its truthfulness upon general experience. But in art, at any rate, the most successful pictures of people are usually portraits of living models, and not phantasies of the artist; and in fiction, too, the truest characters are often representations of their authors, or of their intimate friends. This betrays itself; for when we read a novel of exceptional merit, we say that it is so true and convincing as to seem auto-biographical. Yet the novelist is only a biographer when it suits his convenience; his aim is not that of biography. Quite apart from a very laudable desire to tell a good story (an aspiration rather starved of late), he is concerned with the irrepressible individualism of mankind, with the collision of one mind with another, and with the conflicts that divide a single mind against itself. But if we would follow such commotions to the bitter end, we must find characters more consistent and less yielding than it is natural for people to be; herein lies both the necessity and the dilemma of pure fiction, and it is here too that a good sense of irony may be an inestimable boon to the novelist.

Biographers, until comparatively recent times, were also bothered about the question of consistency, but they were bothered in a different way. There are always plenty of people who deeply mistrust any departure from a rigid consistency; they feel it to be unmanly, if nothing worse. This attitude is at least defensible; what

88

is wrong is that consistency with them is not logically deducible; it is an arbitrary division of things into groups of compatibility, and between the members of different groups there is said to exist the barrier of incompatibility. Such a classification is very largely the product of custom and convention, dependent on the besetting sin of Englishmen, that of over-hasty generalisation. We have ever been hasty in condemning particular actions as belonging to a type of behaviour, to which, under the circumstances, they do not. As we look backwards, this conventionalism, with its corresponding view of consistency, becomes more general; it grows to be identical with respectability. Passing into the eighteenth century, it was perhaps more superficial, but none the less rigid. It was the Englishman's way of fortifying himself against any return of the Restoration debauch, which had become a bogy, and terribly exaggerated at that. It is a curious anomaly that the Puritan spirit, detesting ritual in religion, should nevertheless ritualise ordinary behaviour until freedom was affronted and spontaneity imperilled. A love of ritual, we must suppose, is inherent in human nature; if it is suppressed in church, it will find expression elsewhere.

This attitude was disastrous to biography. Boswell stands out a half-unconscious prophet, whose introductory remarks on biography can never be disregarded without loss. That which brought failure to so many was the secret of his success, an unstinted admiration for his subject. He determined that his picture of Johnson

should be perfect, but he was artist enough to perceive
that you cannot make a picture perfect by the admission
of all defects. The sublimity of human behaviour at its
best lies in the fact that it is an achievement, not to be
continually attained to, and bearing still the marks of
conflict and defectiveness. Dr Johnson was at times
sublime; he was more often content to remain robust,
and not infrequently peevish; and the whole picture is
exceedingly lovable. But in Boswell's time biography
was not consciously admitted to be an art of its own; it
was not disentangled from hero-worship on the one
hand, and the formal 'writing up' of distinguished
careers on the other. Such writers wanted to be fair to
their subject, and they wanted him to appear complete,
his character to display a wholeness; but they fell into
the error of believing consistency (with all the limitations of their special view of it) to be the *sine qua non* of
such a wholeness and such a completeness. In a sense
they were too idealistic, forgetting that an imperfect
race will mistrust anyone of its kind who seems to be
too perfect. At any rate, by omitting much of what
seemed to them inconsistent, and therefore trivial and
irrelevant, in the lives of their subjects, they created
an atmosphere too formal and often too artificial, for
the milder uses of irony; and the same passion for consistency denied its sterner uses, for they forfeited that
opportunity of inductive criticism of mankind which is
always open to the biographer, although too frequent
a use of it would turn a biography into a *post mortem*.
This contingency, however, the eighteenth century

biographers successfully avoided, except, indeed, those revengeful gentlemen who were moved by spite to write uncomplimentary lives of their enemies.

But we will not concern ourselves with them, despite their frequent indulgence in irony; they make good reading on a gloomy afternoon, for they obviously enjoyed themselves. So also did the more genuine biographers, coming up against the detractors of their idols; for sometimes it happened that certain 'inconsistent' facts were too well known to be disregarded, and ill-disposed persons were rashly drawing from these facts the obvious deductions. In such circumstances not only must the hero be afforded an elaborate defence, special circumstances pleaded and ingenious purposes disclosed, but it may be as well to launch against 'the ill-disposed' a modicum of that blind, retributive 'irony,' so irrelevant as to fit any occasion; the 'irony' which calls one's tormentor 'amiable,' which suggests that his fine judgment and unerring memory have on this one occasion failed him; the 'irony' which can convince no one of anything, but may, if he be foolish enough, annoy the person against whom it is directed, and is certainly a convenience for the satisfaction of spleen without positive opprobriousness. We are familiar with it to-day, because it flourishes in hundreds of the letters which week by week extend our daily press; but the most luxuriant growth is to be found in the biographies of the worthies of some two hundred years ago.

The boundary line between sarcasm and the smallest

of ironies is hard to draw, but perhaps our former definition, that in irony the sting must be dependent on truth for its efficacy, will be of assistance here. Such insinuations as we have considered above can never 'to irony pretend'; they lack the edge, the incisiveness that is a property of irony; they are seldom concerned with the exposure of truth, but are often the children of dudgeon and nothing more. The smallest of ironies must strike home; it must win its cause, however trivial. This is where Miss Austen excels; her most playful irony is sometimes the most severe, for she took no risks, and when she employed irony, she did so in perfect confidence; her irony is never tentative.

Such a use of irony will not be found in the biography, or any other literature, of Dr Johnson's time, although he himself sometimes approximated to it, for he had the sense of humour, the whimsicality and power of detachment, which are the antidotes of that 'consistency' complex that hampered biography until Boswell's achievement. Now Johnson's *Lives of the Poets*, although greatly different from what we consider adequate biography to-day, are very important in the history of this subject. The *Lives* exhibit candour and directness, and what is more, there is a true sense of detachment in them, despite the personal prejudices which from time to time appear. They may be wrong-headed, but they are as fair as a wrong head can make them. They are epoch-making in literary criticism, and irony is all along bound up with criticism. But it is significant that in this work Dr Johnson does not greatly employ his irony, indeed it hardly appears at all. The fact is that he regarded biography not, like his predecessors and many of his contemporaries, simply as an honour due to the eminent dead; there was something of public spirit in his book. Biography was the record of their great men that the public had a right to demand; it was history in miniature, the history, not of peoples but of people. But the age which produced Edward Gibbon had a restricted sense of history. History was the science of record; when an historian expresses opinions about the significance of facts he ceases to be an historian; he should only concern himself with establishing their truth. The fact that there is a type of evidence that it takes an artist to perceive, did not occur to them. History was a science, although, of course, in the nature of things it had a strong connection with the art of narrative. Now irony has nothing to do with science, and the art of narrative is purely accessory not only to the science, but also to the art of history and biography.

Boswell has recorded a remark of Johnson's which shows, as clearly as possible, that he held the current view of the historian's task. Yet other things would restrain his irony in the *Lives*, such as his great veneration for poets in general, and his sense of our debt to the past, however imperfect; and why should anyone be ironical, if they do not feel like it? What we are concerned with here is the fact that the scientific, historical element that entered into biography is, taken by itself, just as antipathetic to the use of irony as was the formal admiration of the former period. This 'historical' sense no doubt made the biographer more critical, and increased his sense of detachment. But science, at any rate, cannot criticise life any more than irony can be launched against an inanimate object. For irony is not unmixed with sympathy; it springs from the imagination that understands so well what it dislikes. That is why it is often so bitter; men use it hastily in self-defence to exhaust immediately the early promptings of a sympathy they do not want to entertain. Such irony in one's reflections upon the dead is both unseemly and undignified, and Johnsonian literature is above all else dignified and entirely seemly. But might they not have used that gentler irony which seems almost to continue sympathising, while it criticises? Perhaps they were unable; they felt too deeply and became dumb. They were consistent, and this incongruous thing, this sympathetic disapproval, worried them: it gave them a very peculiar feeling: it must be enthusiasm.

The Romantic Movement reasserted the claims of sympathy over and above criticism. Enthusiasm, reinstated, was impatient for a while of the grave outlook of the age of Johnson. It was all in the air, it had no liveliness. People said it was wide and charitable, but it had no human touch. As time went on, however, the loving subjects of Queen Victoria, just when they were beginning to perceive that they really did love her, may have observed with equanimity the gradual blending of the old and new. But Romanticism approached biography with diffidence, for the mind of the biographer was set; he was still a man with a private mission, or an erector of monuments to the dead and monuments must be grave and solid and dignified, lest a worse thing befall, as our cemeteries bear witness. So Romanticism remained for the most part in the ante-room of the biographer's mind; she might make suggestions about the true nature of hero-worship and deplore the formality of the monumental art, but her sympathy was not a critical sympathy, and it is a good thing that her influence on biography was not greater. Had it been so, the precarious detachment established in Johnson's time must have perished; the truth would have been endangered, not for the sake of consistency but for a less admirable cause, dramatic requirements. As it was, the very gentle touch of the Romantic Spirit brought nothing but gain to biography, for it introduced into it a note of charm hitherto lacking. But the gaze of the biographer was still too exclusively fixed upon his subject, with whom his own mind was synchronised at the beginning, for him to admit the vague disquiet of irony to disturb the serenity of his pages, the serenity that Romanticism had made more precious and, in a sense, more homely. Sympathy and detachment were in the ascendant, but they remained in their separate compartments and seemed to threaten each other. But irony at its best is a child of their union; it arises in the reaction of judgment upon taste, of reflection upon sentiment, and of criticism upon admiration. Such irony as may be found in the mid-Victorian biographies exists outside the mind of the author; from these, as from tombstones and obituary notices, as from the perusal of old letters and diaries, there arises in the mind of the reader a sense of the Irony of Life. Such irony is vague and speculative; it comes when we attempt the impossible, when we seek to look back upon ourselves with the eyes of destiny; it has no certain aim and must needs be content to pity the human race because it is not super-human. But the conscious irony of the mind is critical and directive; it does not seek to gain its ends by transcending human intelligence, but rests with satisfaction upon the secure basis of common sense.

Mrs Gaskell's *Life of Charlotte Brontë* is a good example of mid-Victorian biography at its best. As one reads on, the indomitable spirit of Miss Brontë, when faced with every sort of adversity, excites an increasing admiration. We look at her not from afar but very closely; we stop not to criticise, but to sympathise and applaud her courage. Indeed, she deserves no other treatment. But what is more significant is that the book would not have us stop to reflect, as she must have reflected, upon the unconscious agents of her adversity; to think about the people who were not ill-disposed but did not help; to wonder at that power of absorption that made her father so useless to her. All these things we are led to view almost dispassionately; they are the author's hypotheses, the agents of those circumstances which, we are to observe with delight, are powerless to break Miss Brontë's courageous spirit. Our gaze has been entirely concentrated upon Miss Brontë, with the result that she has not moved amongst living people, rather 'forces' have prowled around her. There can be no irony in such a situation but the empty irony of life.

Mrs Gaskell's *Life of Charlotte Brontë* was published in 1857. If we jump nearly fifty years, we shall find the twentieth century very uncertain of itself, but full of admiration for the greatest literary production of the time—Lord Morley's *Life of Gladstone*. No two lives can be more unlike than the life of a Prime Minister and that of a rather solitary authoress, but the same features may be looked for in the biographical treatment of any life. The experiences of an eminent politician are so manifold and various that they cannot fail to excite, in those who follow them, tangential reflection about the more general themes of human life, and criticisms of the race of man in its complex whole, in addition to the particular analysis of the moment. But in most biographies these reflections spring more naturally from circumstances of the subject's life, from the behaviour of those with whom he had to deal, than from his own behaviour. This is so, because he moves before our gaze so much closer than anyone else; he is the subject, he stands for the particular and lives; the rest may be classified as a single whole; they are the background, they tend to represent the general, and exist, as though they were a Greek chorus. This is useless for irony; the subject is close and sacrosanct; the rest, lifeless and vague. But for the sake of biography, as well as irony, the softening of this distinction should be more seriously attempted than it often is. In this respect biography should more resemble the novel; the subject must not be made less alive, but others must be found to live with him. If he is dethroned only so far as to become A of a group $ABCD$, we shall come to understand him better; he will gain and not lose vitality, for man is a gregarious animal. Very often A will remain close and BCD far away, as it is fitting. But sometimes B or C or D will come closer as A retreats a little, until we look at a more distant A through the eyes of B or C or D; and this, too, is equally fitting, for their view has just as great a claim on our attention as that of the author. Of course, the author remains omnipresent; B is the author's B as A is the author's A; but, even so, the vision will become less restricted, for the author himself reacts differently towards B and C and D, and under such influences may easily catch the A of his original dreams napping.

Such ideal biography is certainly a hard undertaking, and often the necessary materials for it do not exist. But it is a feature of to-day that the biographer has become more ready to smother his feelings and act the spy a little, realising that in so doing he spies not only on his subject but on himself, and also that there can be such a thing as an honest and an amiable spy. This tendency towards the covert look, the vigil round the corner, and the use of the periscope, despite its constant abuse, does at any rate show that people are taking an interest in each other more critical and less hasty in judgment than was the fashion of the preceding age. What looks so like suspicion is often pure curiosity.

So far as irony is concerned this attitude is full of

promise. A slight scepticism, a greater curiosity, a look of science that is not too abstracted, a sympathy that is not too wedded to 'pure feeling'—if these elements that are struggling for expression in modern life can retain their equilibrium, then a golden age of irony will ensue.

Lord Morley was not a great ironist, but his attitude towards his fellows—kindly, inquisitive, analytical, although, as we think, a little heavy-handed, because of some blind spot in his artistic sense, which encouraged his prejudices, such as they were, to take affront—was prophetic of a new age. The *Life of Gladstone* is a landmark in the history of biography. There is no monopoly here of the close look; there are times when Mr Gladstone seems far away, one amongst many of those rather serious and public-spirited Victorians. Some question occupies them, and Mr Gladstone makes his remark. It is a good remark, but why is it slightly amusing? We have a curious feeling, benign, but patronising, rather old and experienced. Did Lord Morley intend this? He has not ostensibly betrayed himself, but the fact remains that he has revealed Mr Gladstone to us, suddenly and without comment, in one of those instances where the Victorian outlook was different from our own, or where his personal idiosyncrasies ran counter to the rules of life demanded by common sense. Here is the Spirit of Irony at work; the Comic Spirit would have sought the aid of Humour; it would dissipate folly with a laugh; while disagreeing, it would heal that disagreement with a caress. But irony refrains from comment; it notes, it accepts and passes on. Yet virtue has gone from it, for that which it has touched remains behind peculiarly naked, and, if it has need to be, ashamed. Such irony is not malicious, for retribution is different from revenge; indeed, there is that about irony which seems almost benignant, for while demolishing them, it delights in the ridiculous and the absurd as affording the spice of life, and the human authors of these follies will not be the worse for its indulgent mockery. But it is without positive kindness; it sympathises, so to speak, without emotion; and what it has laid bare it will not cover up again, for it believes that no good thing is the worse for fresh air and the light of day. Only with what is unpleasant it adopts a sterner tone, involving more completely the person in the condemnation of the act.

The progress of such irony will be precarious; especially in biography, where prejudice is insistent. Yet since 1903, when Lord Morley's *Life of Gladstone* was published, it has taken a firmer root in our biography at the hands of living authors whose names it will be unnecessary to mention, but whom the reader will call to mind. It is sufficient here to add that, despite their successes, our modern ironists have not altogether avoided the Scylla and Charybdis between which true irony disports itself; 'cleverness' on the one hand, and spitefulness on the other. But their success is greater than their failure; the only danger is that fashion will bring disaster by outrunning necessity.

In conclusion, it may be well to point out that in this section, as indeed throughout this book, we have been more concerned with the general progress of literature than with particular works of great merit, which for that very reason stand somewhat outside their own times. We have attempted to trace the development of the art of biography only so far as that art is concerned with an understanding and a use of irony. But in any age there will always be some exceptional men whose works seem to belie the unfortunate writer who is forced by circumstance into the rashness of generalisation. In this particular connection Hogg's *Life of Shelley* might be taken as one example amongst many others. This remarkable book, appearing at the moment when the romantic veneration for Shelley was at its zenith, contains just that frankness and many-sidedness that was largely lacking in contemporary biography. It also possesses an haphazard attention to detail that is very illuminating. Hogg was, in some ways, a wild and undisciplined Boswell. Yet this book is an argument for, rather than against, our contentions; for, published as late as 1858, it nevertheless so shocked contemporary opinion as to what was appropriate in a biographer, that Hogg was dissuaded from continuing his work, and his biography of Shelley ends with the poet's elopement with Mary Godwin.

III

HISTORY

It might be expected that the place of the historian amongst ironists would be an important one, for the perusal of the past is well calculated to engender an ironical frame of mind. However great his natural optimism, the historian must be greatly concerned with the errors, the miscalculations, and the wilfulness of mankind. The inveterate selfishness of our species is the general topic of all history, while a peculiar denseness and obstinacy of disposition is the particular phenomenon which, we are told, demands the attention of English historians. In addition to this there is much in the circumstances of being an historian which ought to encourage irony. The biographer is concerned with a single character, usually not far removed from his own times; the historian is, as it were, suspended in a balloon over the world of some past age; there is much that he can see clearly and much that eludes his gaze, and changes in the historical weather disturb from time to time both his composure and his view. But despite these difficulties he can discover many things. He can observe, for instance, innumerable cases where the future derides men's hopes and mocks their conceptions. The conscious efforts of men are often doomed to insignificance in the course of history, while their unconscious achievements are sometimes fraught with great potentialities, which, in the fullness of time, blossom into positive force. In the same way hasty and careless decisions may supply what heroism has sought to obtain in vain. These are the larger incongruities of history, the smaller are legion; there are the inconsistencies of those who gloried especially in consistency, the fallibilities of those who thought themselves infallible; the honours which adorned the empty-headed and the disregard which has seemed so often to crown the lives of great men. Such things cannot escape the historian; sometimes they monopolise his attention and the reader wearies of his lamentations over the shortcomings of man and the vagaries of fortune; others are less prodigal of comment, but spoil the occasion for it by an excursion into high matters touching the blindness of fate. The advantage to the historian of a judicious irony in such cases is considerable, for irony relieves an author of the necessity of making a direct comment which it would be difficult to achieve without heaviness or, at least, a lack of grace. There are many cases where the historian desires to suggest something which it would be tedious to enlarge upon; yet he does not like it to escape the reader's mind, and, author-like, mistrusts the power of others to draw it, unhelped and unsolicited, from the bare facts. Now that magic of words whereby so much 'more is meant (and said) than meets the eye' is the result of the general art of writing which we call style. But in narrative, and especially in history, which is critical narrative, it partakes of the ironic character of Burke's oratorical *meiosis*. Criticism, or mere comment, may for convenience be made inherent in narrative; it may also be condensed in this way because its strength and cogency will be thereby increased. We are all familiar with passages in the Bible, especially in the Gospel narrative, where the power of such restraint reveals itself; and when that which is left unmentioned, but not unexpressed, belongs to the sphere of criticism, we feel the ironic spirit to be at work.

Such a use of irony makes the most exacting demands upon literary skill; be it a little too gentle it may escape the reader's notice; but too harsh an irony has far worse consequences, for not only does it arouse the reader's indignation against the author himself, but it prejudices his mind against that very sentiment which it had been intended the irony should convey. Yet, amongst English historians, there have been great stylists of whom it would be hard to believe that they neglected irony because they felt incompetent to use it; far more likely is the cause to be found in temperament. We venture to believe that the Englishman is, more than most men, a partisan. Supreme partisanship has, as often as not, been the main incentive which, consciously or unconsciously, has goaded the Englishman into writing the history of his country. Clarendon and Macaulay are two very different instances of this. To both of these men lack of political detachment denied the best uses of irony in history; the necessary restraint would have been impossible for either of them. It is, therefore, equally sensible of Clarendon to indulge in straightforward criticism of his opponents, that is frequently not without dignity, and of Macaulay to allow the spirit of Romance to soften the bitterness of cleavages that were revived with such acerbity in his own lifetime. The partisan cannot with impunity avail himself of the irony that belongs more truly to the prophet. The case of Clarendon, who was writing contemporary history, is naturally extreme, but the uninterrupted evolution of our institutions makes English history, at any rate from the Civil Wars onwards, comparatively recent history. It would be exceedingly difficult for an enthusiastic Whig of Macaulay's time not to carry both his enthusiasms and his hatreds back into the reign of Queen Anne. How prone we are to do this, and to transport our own outlook into the past, to the detriment both of truth and fairness may be seen from the errors of the historical school which is connected with the name of Freeman; and even Stubbs, whose science and detachment enabled him to reconstruct on a firmer basis the early history of England, himself in the company of the Ecclesiastical Commissioners of 1895, fell a victim to the *idée fixe* and needed the kindly correction of Maitland. Controversial irony is not a particularly attractive form of irony, and is not in any way the exclusive property of history. Maitland, however, who should be numbered among the great stylists who have written our history, is not without an admirable sense of irony, which manifests itself in his works of historical criticism. Always gentle and humorous, it is often based upon the juxtaposition of some modern theory with the sayings and actions of the people of the past with whom that theory is concerned. In this way he saves himself much tedious argument and logical construction: it is the old method of *reductio ad absurdum* used with elegance and tact. Thus the elliptic properties of irony are as useful and convincing in historical criticism as elsewhere, but it takes a great man to use them with complete fairness, and not to pervert the issue by an undue eclecticism in the selection of material as evidence; and the greater a man's art in writing, the more seductive will the vivacious qualities of irony prove. Maitland, at any rate, emerges from this test with honour.

If partisanship encumbers the Englishman recording the history of his own country, perhaps in the history of other nations we shall see him at his best, and shall find there that broad and unbiassed historical outlook wherein we are endeavouring to find the place of irony. It is sometimes said that history unprompted by partisanship or by any special motive becomes no longer an art but simply a collection of scientific data; that a man either writes history to support his creed, whatever it may be (in which case he is not writing true history), or simply produces bricks to build the palaces of anthropology and political science. But to the simpleminded, that is a strange perversion of the truth: history is simply the record of human life, and if life is a romance, history must be so too; if there is art in life, there is art in history; we cannot dissociate the record of behaviour altogether from the effect of that behaviour on the minds of those who read the record. This is not irrelevant; for if the holders of the scientific theory are in the right, the historian who makes use of irony ceases at that moment to be an historian. But the whole argument is a matter of definition of terms; is a table what I think of in my mind as a table, or so many pounds of wood in a particular shape? To the average man a table stands for what it does, not what it is. What history has always done is to interest men's minds and stimulate their enthusiasms. Anthropology and political science to-day go as far as anything in prompting historical research, but their claims to begin with, at any rate, were felt but vaguely: they were an added interest, or more truly, a specialised part of the general interest arising from history, enlivening the products of a more simple conception. This conception is that history is the account of men's successive efforts to obtain freedom and happiness. It becomes an epic rather than a chronicle. If it were in this spirit only that historians have written we should expect to find in their work evidences of that wide and serene outlook that is doubly indulgent and doubly censorious, reserving both praise and blame for motive rather than achievement, observing the interplay of design and circumstances and the influence, often insidious enough, of mental abstraction. There is scope for the true ironist, passing judgment undisturbed by the importunate claims of the fetishes of any age.

Lord Acton possessed, perhaps, more than anyone since his time, this vision and this power of irony. His published works are few, consisting in the main of lectures and short essays. He was seldom the deliberate wielder of irony, but his unerring presentation of facts is constantly producing in the reader's mind that sense of the false relations of things, which the circumstances of normal life so easily present to the unwary, of the disparity between what is happening and what men think is happening. In his *Lectures on Modern History* it seems to us that Lord Acton carries the art of compressed narrative to a very high standard.

There is always a prophetic zeal, however disciplined, in his work, for Lord Acton was an ardent apostle of freedom and tolerance. Very different is Edward Gibbon, who alone has equalled him in breadth of historic vision. Gibbon is *par excellence* the stylist amongst English historians, but he is also the greatest ironist of them all. In the anthology which no one has published of Gibbon's history, there might be three divisions. The first section would contain the brilliant epigrams— description, comparison, and valuation pressed into a single sentence; the second would supply examples of that triumphant cynicism and wilful scepticism that are saved by the humour which so often belies them; in the third section there would be found those passages where the whole trend, significance and worth of events is submitted to a penetrating and masterly summary. In all three sections the hand of irony would be observed frequently at work, but whereas the first two would reveal the trivial, if amusing, irony of the brilliant writer and clever cynic, in the last there would appear the irony that is born of true detachment and unrivalled clear-sightedness. No one has viewed the world from a more solitary and commanding position than that to which Gibbon climbed to command the Roman Empire; and from that height he awakens in his readers a recognition of the incongruities of things, and in this recognition both the true and relative values of the incongruous are momentarily and suddenly clear. This is the true work of irony, not the scourging and the lashing, but simply the laying bare. It is not the irony that is characteristically English, not prophetic irony, but the irony of the clear-sighted and dispassionate observer. It contains the common factor of all ironic experience, of the so-called irony of life, of dramatic irony, and of the critical irony that belongs to speech and letters. It belongs to genius and not to nations, and with it and a tribute to Edward Gibbon we may most suitably bring this inadequate survey to a close.

For EU product safety concerns, contact us at Calle de José Abascal, 56–1°, 28003 Madrid, Spain or eugpsr@cambridge.org.

www.ingramcontent.com/pod-product-compliance
Ingram Content Group UK Ltd.
Pitfield, Milton Keynes, MK11 3LW, UK
UKHW020312140625

459647UK00018B/1845